WARP AND WOOF

A BOOK OF VERSE

BY

SAMUEL WILLOUGHBY DUFFIELD

Spin, spin, Clotho, spin!
 Lachesis, twist! and Atropos, sever!
Darkness is strong, and so is Sin,
 But only God endures forever.

LOWELL.

NEW YORK:
ANSON D. F. RANDOLPH & CO.,
770 BROADWAY.
1870.

WARP AND WOOF

A BOOK OF VERSE

BY

SAMUEL WILLOUGHBY DUFFIELD

Spin, spin, Clotho, spin!
  Lachesis, twist! and Atropos, sever!
Darkness is strong, and so is Sin,
  But only God endures forever.

LOWELL.

NEW YORK:
ANSON D. F. RANDOLPH & CO.,
770 BROADWAY.
1870.

Warp and Woof

A BOOK OF VERSE

BY

SAMUEL WILLOUGHBY DUFFIELD

Spin, spin, Clotho, spin!
Lachesis, twist! and Atropos, sever!
Darkness is strong, and so is Sin,
But only God endures forever.

Lowell.

NEW YORK:
ANSON D. F. RANDOLPH & CO.,
770 BROADWAY.
1870.

To One Nearest and Dearest

and

to those other

True and Faithful Hearts

who love me

and whom I love

I Dedicate

whatever of good these pages

may contain

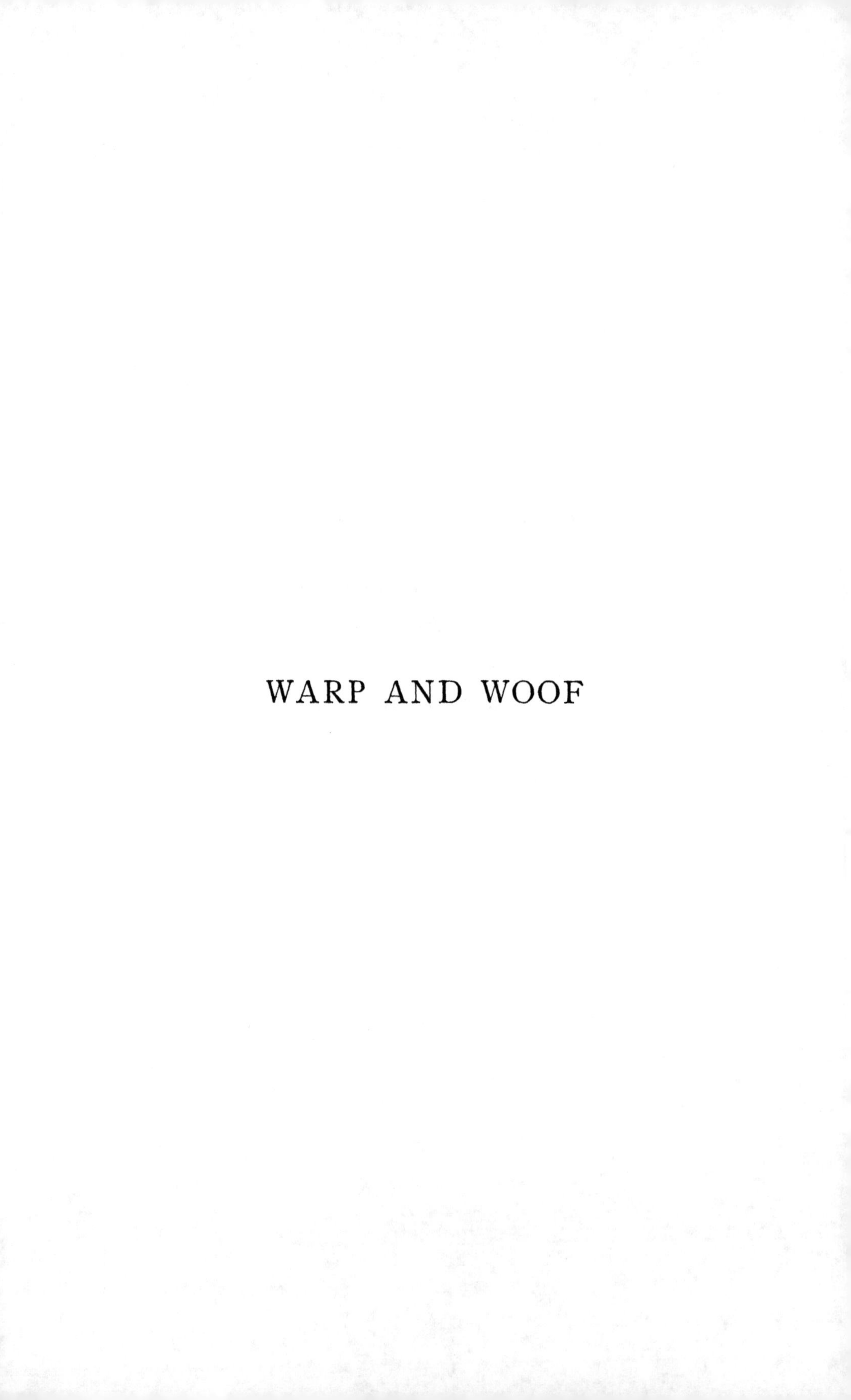

WARP AND WOOF

SAMPLE CARD.

WOVEN AT ODD HOURS.

WOVEN ON QUIET DAYS.

SHREDS AND TAGS.

AT THE LOOM.

HAST thou, then, a plentiful store
  Of wit and wisdom and art divine?
Lovest thou mystery all the more,
  Because in its bosom the truth doth shine?
Art thou broad in thy brains and brow?—
Merry companion of mine art thou.

Dost thou see in a little thing,
  Blossom or berry, or forest leaf,
Falling in Fall or rising in Spring,
  A legend or tragedy writ in brief?
Are thine eyes on such pages now?—
Merry companion of mine art thou.

Canst thou sing to the nested bird,
  Chirrup with crickets, or hum with bees,
Live with them in their life, unstirred
  By frivolous fashions, among the trees?
Doth thy sympathy these allow?—
Merry companion of mine art thou.

Hadst thou sooner behold the red
  Shining up by the mountain's crest,

Breathing freshness from overhead,
And talking with Nature at her best?
Sooner this than a magnate's bow?—
Merry companion of mine art thou.

Dost thou love with a poet's love
Beauty of sky and beauty of sea,
Beauty in field and beauty in grove,
Beauty on lake, and beauty on lea?
Loves like these never fade, I trow:
Merry companion of mine art thou.

Thou and I through the livelong day,
Gathering fancies out of the world,
Plucking pictures—shall stroll and stray
In every nook where a song is curled:
Bound with me in a common vow,
Merry companion of mine art thou.

WOVEN FROM OLD THREADS.

ATALANTA AND HIPPOMENES.

UPON the yellow margin of the sea
By hollow-footed surges trampled down,
Full in the strong breath of the salt, swift breeze,
Arcadian Atalanta chose the lists.
Divine she stood, at ease amid the throng,
With golden hair in wavy lines blown back,
And golden quiver slung across her arm
In careless grace — one quick, high-arching foot
Beating impatience on the sodden sand
Which gathered into moisture at her tread.

One while she looked beyond the broken surf,
And saw white sails against the azure sky
And flaking foam hurled high by many oars,
And listened to their pulsing roll which beat
Responsive to the beating of her heart;
Then turned upon a curious, twisted shell,
With myriad whorls like Minos' labyrinth
Afar in Crete — caught it, and cast it off
Among the combing breakers inward bound,

And laughed to see it skip and plunge and sink;
A cruel laugh — a hard, disdainful laugh,
Self-confident, and bitter as the sea.

The elders marked the course — slowly along
The hard, firm margin pacing with a care
On which hung life and death. Two willow wands
Peeled silver-white they fixed at either end;
And then, in the great hush of coming fate,
When men breathe hard and none may dare to speak,
They took their stations sadly and in fear.
And then Hippomenes, the chosen judge,
Rose up and, stately, strode into the midst.

And the high gods looked from the sky that day
Upon the maiden, snowy-pure and cold
As desolate peaks — upon the long sea-reach —
Upon the eager suitors, hungry-eyed
With gazing at the fairness to be won —
Upon the mute, attentive throng, who crept
Closer together as the moment came,
And who, in that fair face, only beheld
The death which threatened to all lagging feet.

Aye, she was beautiful, this huntress maid,
This princess light and bright, whose ready hand
Twanged well-wrought bow-strings after flying deer;
Whose foot outwent the hounds of Thessaly;
Whose eye was keener than the falcon's glance;
Whose lifted spear made men to stand aghast
And reel affrighted from the fiend which held

Possession of that unrelenting face.
Aye, she was goddess-like, white-armed and poised
In truest balance of divinity:
But under these were hid the unexplored
Deep harmonies which tremble in men's lives —
Chords needing but a master-hand to strike
That they might tell, instead of woes and wars,
Of love which swept these lesser notes aside,
And rose, once sounded, over all the rest.

To her a fearful saying, boding grief,
Came once with warning: "Marry not, O maid,
For wedlock shall be ruin." So, alone,
Tempting the furthest fastness of the woods,
She moved serene in joys of open air,
And scorned to hear a word of tenderness.

Until, reluctant, to appease the men
Who sought her hero-wise and gave and took
Great blows to gain her favor, and who kept
Track of the ground she walked on, worshipping,
As though the woodland goddess, Artemis,
Had taken on such guise to tread the earth;
She found this one condition which she used:
Whoever held himself her worthy mate
Must prove as well her equal in the race;
But, if Defeat ran grimly at his heels
And clutched him round the heart and broke his
strength,
He should receive, in token of her faith,
Death by the sword — and unto this she kept

So deadly true, that many failed thereat,
And died because of love and lack of speed.
For she was swifter than an eagle's flight
Through the broad heaven; so light of step was she
That none might seek to vie with her and live.

The perfect day shone on without a cloud;
And men kept silent, waiting for the end;
While still was heard the ripple of the brine
Trundling discarded shells upon the beach,
And waters breaking in monotonously.
Still did the galleys with their brazen prows
Cleave the high ocean-swells and leap along,
The shields of heroes flashing from their sides –
Still did the pitiless glory of the sun
Irradiate that strip of fateful shore —
Still in his hand, as yet aloft in air,
Hippomenes displayed the judge's staff,
Whose fall should be the signal for the race —
And the high gods still watched from overhead,
Seeing what labors men endure for love.

But Aphrodite, goddess of the foam,
To whom belongs the frothing of the wine
And all the bubbling of the cup of youth,
Infused Hippomenes with strong desire
Himself to test his chances for the maid.
Yet was he calm withal, and bore his place;
Delaying, that the first hard strife might cease.

The moment came — a single downward stroke
Of hand and truncheon, and they bounded off,

Tearing the matted sand with naked feet;
While full in front, with tresses on the breeze,
And springing step which put their best to shame,
Arcadian Atalanta led the van,
Supremely swift, as when a falling star
Trails its long, fiery hair against the night.
Then backward, like a lioness aroused
She darted, giving orders, and the guards
Seized on those luckless lords, and dragged them off,
And slew them with the sword, not sparing one —
Inflicting grief upon the throng around.
While she who did it all — a trifle flushed,
With breath which came and went a motion more
Than when of old she stood upon the strand —
Seemed to Hippomenes far lovelier
Than any maiden of the maids of Greece.

Descending from his station, with a prayer
To Aphrodite, who had urged his soul,
He strode in front, and bending royally
Before the daughter of Iäsius,
Kinglike he spoke, and proffered to essay
Against her, for the prize herself had set,
Another contest such as was the last:
"For he had sooner die and perish soon
Slain in such wise, than drag a weary life,
Forgotten and forsaken, through the world."

The princess looked and saw a proper man,
Right regal in the fashion of his strength,
With mighty sinews, features of that brown

Which is the guerdon of the healthful sun
When wine-cups redden not and all is pure;
And seeing, loved — for so ordained the queen
Who sways our hearts however she may choose.

On the one hand the solemn Parcæ stood,
With thread and weft and shears to clip the skein,
Which is the tangled semblance of our days;
While on the other tarried, beckoning,
Idalian Aphrodite, turning back
With an entreating, wistful tenderness,
Before she left her lonely on the earth.
He was too brave to die; and yet, alas!
None may withstand the Fates. If it might be
That he was victor, she could lose her pride
And take the future as a cheerful lot.

But he with gesture and with hasty word
Repelled his friends who gave discouragement,
Since unto him a presence, viewless, sweet,
With rich, soft breath compact of odors rare,
Diffusing pleasure, had approached. It spoke
Some low, clear words; and though he might not catch
A glimpse of deity, he felt its proof
In that which came from thence a gift to him:
For three bright apples, grown from choicest gold,
On golden boughs, with golden leaves for shade,
In gardens of her own, the goddess brought
Unseen, and thrust them underneath his robe,
With whispered words of comfort; and the crowd
(As is the manner of prosaic souls)

Deemed only that some hardier wind had blown
A burst of inland perfume over them!

And then advanced a man of snowy beard,
Who drew one short, deep furrow in the sand
With his staff's point, and, mourning in his heart,
Made signal of a preparation closed.
And they passed steadily toward their goal
Expectant, pausing at the place assigned;
While strong and loud and ringing like the clang
Of sword on shield burst forth the final word.

No whirlwind hurrying through the desert dunes
So dashed and threw the sand, as these who flew
O'er the sea-margin, hurling far away
Wet, clinging particles from flying feet.
Shoulder by shoulder, pace for pace they sped,
Scaring the mussels stranded on the coast;
Making the crabs slip sideways to the sea;
Frighting the sail-winged gulls from idleness
And easy circling after finny spoil;
Holding uplifted heads against the sharp,
Refreshing saltness of the breath of spray,
Either intent to win; until it chanced
That Atalanta gained the foremost place,
And set a spear's-length as the space between.
For then Hippomenes with sudden force
Flung a bright apple, yellow-hued and fair,
Gleaming and dazzling with supernal light,
Athwart her and beyond, toward the cliffs.
And then the maiden, pausing, caught it up—
But yet came after, and went bounding by.

Another sphere of gold he cast aside
Into the very edges of the surf,
And Cytherea, hovering close, impelled
The Arrow-Footed to attain the prize;
While still her suitor pressed undaunted on,
For now the flickering line of silver-white
Pointed the utmost limit near at hand.

Again the damsel, like the blinding bolt
Of summer lightning, passed him in the course;
And he, with fear of death before his eyes,
Cast hope and trust and confidence away
With his last apple, fairer than the rest.
Full to the side he threw it, as he sprang
Across the intervening stretch of shore,
With quick, hard-gathered breath and parching lips
And muscles quivering from overtask.
Full to the side the maiden swerved in chase,
And he swept on, successful, to the goal.

Then was there joy throughout the Grecian land;
And mellow piping upon tuneful reeds;
And songs and jests and dances in the shade;
And games and gladsome days and gayety.
The realm was left forgotten of its lord;
The hounds, forsaken by their huntress-queen,
Went wretchedly in couples up and down;
The spear leaned idly rusting in its nook;
The bow lay bent, the arrows strewn around,
The buskins tossed aside. The forest stood
Amid its thickets, silent as at first

Before its glades re-echoed with the horn.
And they, for whom the land was jubilant,
Found an oblivion of sweet delight
Securely resting in each other's arms;
Comprising, in themselves and in their joy,
A world in which the dwellers were but two.

Until that fate, which follows all mankind,
Pursued them both, and sent Cybele there;
For, careless in their love, they ceased to pay
Due reverence to other than themselves,
And thus called down a vengeance from on high.
With fatal wrath she visited their sin;
And now, their human figure laid aside,
Transformed to lion and to lioness,
Yoked to her car they drag her through the vales—
For so the faith of oracles is kept.

SARPEDON.

. . . . "Ubi ingens
Sarpedon." . . . .

DEAD, on the plain before the walls of Troy;
Dead, in the shadows of the setting sun;
Stripped of his royal armor — desolate —
No more the stay of Priam and his house —
He lies alone, among the fallen Greeks.

Him, in his pride, well-greaved Patroclus slew,
And sent his soul to Hades, with the throng
Of valiant Argives conquered by his hand.
Alas, Sarpedon! whom we called the Great —
Mighty of spirit, mightier in strength,
And mightiest in birth from Zeus supreme —
Had I but died with thee!
O gallant heart,
That gave thyself to save a ruined race!
O victor through defeat! — may it be well
Among Elysian fields by Lethe's bank!

. . . .

The golden horses of the sun had passed
Beyond the red horizon's dimmest edge;
And Phœbus, bending from the chariot,
Majestic, robed in light, with naked arm
Pointed toward the East, and motioned still
As if to give command.

And then there came
Between the glory of the setting sun
And us, the shadow of an awful dark;
And in it were two forms — one pale and wan,
With sunken cheeks, and hollow eyes, and hands
That grasped beyond it, clutching at the air;
The other dim and dusky, indistinct,
Shrouded in mystery, yet friendlier
In all that might be viewed of mien and look
Than that first dreadful figure.
Hovering
Along the borders of the lower air,
They sank to earth where great Sarpedon lay
Still, in the trampled dust; and then one said,
"To Lycia!" and pointed with his hand
As did Apollo — and they took him up
Between them, and I knew that awful shape
Whom men call Death, and dread to look upon;
And that mysterious one, dim, dusky Sleep,
His own twin brother.
Swifter than the speed
Of Hermes, messenger of Zeus, they flew;
Yet tenderly, as one would a sick child,
They bore the great Sarpedon to his rest
Among the Lycians, by the tideless sea.

"LEYDEN, A. D. 1574."

UPON the stubborn anvil of our fate
We fashion out the metal that we are,
Baser or finer as the test shall prove.
And he who has endured the hottest flame,
Comes forth most tractable, and so is worked
Into what form shall please the Master best.
It is the souls which bear most fearful scars
Whom God delights to honor, and whose place
Is nearest to Him on the trial day.
Much has been granted to them, and their love
Is greater than of those who suffered less;
For so the unseen purpose keeps its ground
Beside the furnace when it glows the most,
And, if we will but see it, leaves us not
To perish in the fierceness of the heat.
Thus may we, in the struggle of our lives,
Move ever upward, till we break and leave
The dross which wrapped us closest at the first.

Through every life may run a thread of faith,
On which, as on a necklace, day by day,
It may be ours to string the benisons
Of God, the Only Wise, and thus obtain
The perfect riches of another world,
Which neither fail nor fade — whose glory-light
Takes lustre from the smile of Him who reigns
Forever and forever, and whose eyes
Count nothing holy which is void of Him.

There have been those of every age and clime,
Men who have wrestled strongly with themselves,
Who, beating down all pride and self-conceit,
Stood forth in might which was not of the earth;
Men who have faced the fagot and the stake,
Conquered the rack, and even from their foes
Won the unwilling tribute of a tear;
Men who have borne the hatred of the world,
Despised its honors, and in spurning them
Gained threefold praises; men whose hopes were set
In one grand thought of duty unto God.

Such are the names upon the scroll of fame
In golden letters, as the Saxon king
Wrote for his people's guidance and his own.
Such are the deeds at which we pause and ask
If these were truly men, so highly stand
Their meekness, patience, courage, over ours;
Such are the way-lights flashing in the past,
With gleams which cheer the darkness.

And of these
There is no nobler record than is left
Of one poor burgher of the Netherlands,
Whose story I have brought you here to-day.

Buttressed back by weary labor from the sea which roars around,
In a land where dauntless courage hallowed every foot of ground,
Still secure in sturdy freedom are the walls of Leyden found.

Through it still the Rhine stream wanders, and the gardens scent the air,
And the tower of Hengist lowers, and the orchards blossom fair;
While the river, winding slowly, nets the houses everywhere.

Round it still the traces cluster of a battle nobly fought,
Held in memory by tokens which a patient valor wrought,
Kept in trust for future ages, sacred unto grateful thought.

It was when the Spaniard Valdez, with his troops in full array,
Marched against its walls and turrets, that the burghers stood at bay,
Choosing rather siege and famine, than the loss of right to pray.

It was when the Spaniard Valdez, looking over lake and town,
Gathered unto him his army, and, to win it for the crown,
Fronting on the gates of Leyden settled all his cannon down.

Then the Holland blood dashed faster, pulsing firmly from the heart;

Then the oath went up to Heaven, Never from their
rights to part;
Then the true and only courage into life began to
start.

And to one stout burgomaster (governor by right
and choice)
Came a greeting in the tumult, even like an angel's
voice,
Bidding him in all the darkness prove his fitness to
rejoice.

Adrian Van Werf of Leyden, fought the foes that
stirred within,
Conquering the evil counsels which denied that he
could win —
Clinched the bolt of honest purpose as the people
drove it in.

Adrian Van Werf of Leyden, with his trust in God
and right,
Double-barred the city portals and made ready for
the fight,
Looking for a glorious morning after long and
dreary night.

Adrian Van Werf of Leyden, seeing that which
needs must come,
Summoned all his townsmen round him at the beat-
ing of the drum;
And in word of doubt or chiding every citizen was
dumb.

So the message flew that evening, as the sunlight grew more pale,
Borne to William, Prince of Orange, as he fretted in his mail,
"For three months we hold the city. Aid us, lest we starve and fail!"

We only know ourselves and learn
The recess hidden in the dark,
When, lurid through the night, we mark
The martyr-flames and torches burn.

Cast on our fate, we rise and strive
Unaided, in the combat grim,
While moon and stars grow sadly dim,
And hope but just remains alive.

Ah, how the armor-joints are tried,
How fast and fell the sword-strokes fall!
And if this life alone were all,
It were as pleasure to have died.

But here and there within the heart
That seems the feeblest, burst and bloom
Some germs of courage from the gloom
Too pure for any human art.

To stand and face the death which comes
Inevitable, and be true
To that which has been set to do,
Amid the rattle of the drums;

When faith in man has failed, when he,
  In whom we fix our firmest trust,
  Yields bitterly, a thing of dust,
And owns his purpose may not be;

And still to fight, when borne above
  The hostile camp fly words that weep
  For helpless sympathy, and keep
No expectation but of love;

This is to be a man indeed,
  And this, when hope is undermined,
  Is that supporting force behind,
Which equals the impelling need.

But men may fall and gently pass
  From toil to triumph in the skies,
  As some soft vapor breaks and flies
From the dimmed surface of a glass.

And so they fell within the wall.
  Spared by the sword that slew without,
  They died with no brave battle-shout—
Death's famine clutches on them all.

The phantom strode along the street,
  Unwearied with his horrid task,
  And men forgot at length to ask
For those whom they were wont to meet.

All traffic ceased, the loaded wain
  Stood useless by the empty stalls,
  For they who fortified the walls
Had other thoughts than those of gain.

Death was as near as Life. It slept
  Beside the warder on the wall;
  It bore the corpse, without a pall,
Unto a nameless grave, unwept.

And still no cheerful message came,
  To tell of dikes just hewn away;
  Of waters seeking for their prey;
For week by week was still the same.

This awful stillness of despair,
  This dreadful strength of iron will,
  Held firm the city portals still,
And kept the flag aloft in air.

But eagerly the eyes were turned
  On Hengist's tower, by night and day,
  For thence a watcher gazed alway,
Whose glances on the distance burned.

And if the booms were broken down,
  And if the fleet should yet appear,
  He would proclaim, in words of cheer,
The speedy succor of the town.

Insultingly the Spaniards threw
  Their letters on a cross-bow shaft.
  Defiantly the burghers laughed,
And hurled their challenge forth anew.

While Adrian Van Werf — as pale
  As any spectre from the tomb —
  Stalked ever on amid the gloom,
And bade them die, but never fail.

And there were some who now and then
  Broke up the silence with a strain
  Of music, uttered forth with pain,
To raise the spirit of the men.

And women, weak and faint and wan,
  Crept forth in groups, and listened there
  To words which seemed a very prayer,
As songs like this came floating on: —

"If that our Lord be for us,
  Who then shall triumph o'er us?"

  Ah, but in doubt and anguish,
  Often and oft we languish.

  Dark is our sky with vapors,
  Faint are these feeble tapers.

  Poor are our lives and earthy,
  And of His love unworthy.

Father, be Thou beside us,
Comfort and stay and guide us.

Thou who art ever near us,
Shed all Thy light to cheer us.

So shall we never perish,
If but Thy love we cherish;

And each upright endeavor
Thou wilt reward forever.

Or else a poet from the throng
Retired awhile to stay his grief,
And sought and found a sure relief
In the sweet cadences of song.

And thus he blessed his magic art,
So pure, so holy, and so true;
And at the morning in the dew,
Forgot the pain which filled his heart: —

Three brothers passed me on their way
Across the meadows rich and green,
To where the distant hills were seen
This summer day.

One caught his carol from the bird,
And, humming as he walked along,
Poured forth upon the air a song,
The sweetest heard.

Another snatched a forest leaf,
  And on it graved strange woodland things,
  And clouded it with flitting wings,
    As fair and brief.

The third looked on them both and smiled,
  Then wove the melody of birds,
  And rustic pictures, into words
    As pure and mild.

And while they moved beyond recall,
  I said within my heart of hearts,
  "They well have learned their noble arts;
    God shield them all!"

But there was one who heard the minstrel's rhyme,
Whose faith in God grew lofty and sublime;
Who trod the ramparts, scanning where below
Lay the white-tented city of the foe.
Despair, which ruled the others, had not shown
That she could make this sturdy soul her own.
The people met him, raising their thin hands,
With squalid faces, querulous demands;
And mothers lifted babes about to die
To meet the stern old burgomaster's eye.
They cried for food, they threatened to unbar
Those gates from which recoiled the tide of war.
They cursed the Prince of Orange, and the State
Which left them thus, unheeded, to their fate.

They clamored loudest for their share of bread,
And wondered much from whence they should be fed.
They roused from stupor when they saw him near,
And dinned expostulations in his ear.
What! would he have them perish for the sake
Of one poor town, one single shallow lake?

Until his spirit, true against the foe,
Was almost broken at his townsmen's woe;
And yet he dared not call the Spaniard in,
Or make concession to the Man of Sin.
He freely offered all that he possessed,
To furnish any comfort to the rest.
He bore the same and shared alike the toil;
Aimed the great gun and dug the heavy soil;
Watched through the night, arose betimes to pray,
And in adventurous forays led the way.
All this he did, but never would unclose
The gates of Leyden to her Romish foes.
Firm in the right, he could not turn aside
For pain, for passion, or for human pride.

The vivid lightning purifies the air;
The fiercest tempest brings the grass to life;
The finest fruit repays the cruel care
Of tortured branches and the pruner's knife.

And we whom God has set amid the world,
Who bow before the storm and dread its force,
Whom oftentimes the hurricane has hurled
Beyond the limits of its utmost course; —

We who are scathed, and gnarled, and warped, and
wrenched;
Whose fruit the canker-worm of pride destroys;
Around whose roots the fire but now is quenched;
Who dare not raise green temples and rejoice; —

We who are all unworthy of His thought,
Receive of Him the bounty of His hand,
And with our inmost fibres are enwrought
The sustenance He gives us from the land.

He will not suffer us to fade and die
If we but reach to Him in feebleness.
He hears our faintest, most despairing cry,
And holds us — ready even then to bless.

Ah, coward hearts! that doubt and doubt again,
Because His way is not the way we seek,
Because the purpose of the Lord is plain,
And words of His are not as mortals speak.

What then are we, that, circled by our fate,
We should adventure other ways than His,
Should strive to hew us out another gate
To realms beyond, avoiding that which is?

For though we seem at times shut closely in
By walls of Providence which hem the sky,
We have no warrant that our cause shall win,
If we permit His cause to pass us by.

And thus was he of Leyden, for he knew
No other guidance than had led him on —
No other one to whom his heart was true;
No other service but of God alone.

Thus glided by the days, and still the plague
Stalked hand-in-hand with famine in the street —
A fearful phantom; strange, and weird, and vague,
At which men's pulses ceased at once to beat.

Meanwhile the missives from the Prince could give
No token of the rising of the waves;
Sick unto death he lay at Rotterdam,
And all the dikes loomed grimly as before.
Unless the waters rose and swept the plain
There was no shade of hope, and thus anew
The people round their leader clamored on.
And once he turned, tall, haggard, dark of face,
Noble in mien, and nobler still in soul,
And men could not endure his steady eye.
"What would you, friends?" he cried. "Why murmur ye
Because we keep our vows, and do not yield,
As yet, unto the tyranny of Spain?
This fate is horrible; but this to that
Would be as dust in balance. I that speak
Have made an oath to hold the city free,
And may the Lord, to whom I pledge myself,
Grant strength to keep my oath. I can but die,
And die but once. I care not if it be
By you, or by the enemy, or God.

Whatever may befall, it moves me not;
But Leyden's fate is dearer than my own.
Soon we shall starve and perish, if relief
Does not appear. And yet, dishonored death —
That death which follows from dishonored life —
Is worse than famine. Threat me if you like.
Take this poor life — I leave it in your hands.
Here is my sword — plunge this within my breast —
Divide my body for your share of food;
But, while I live, surrender shall not be.
Expect it not, for it will never come."

Famished and fainting as they were, they rose
In tenfold courage, and a shout went up
That rang defiance to the Spanish camp.
And then once more ascending tower and roof,
And peering from the battered battlements,
They hurled renewed invective on the foe;
Watching afar the courses of the streams,
To view if Father Ocean sent them aid.

. . . .

While Adrian Van Werf went home to pray,
And laid his bitter burden on the Lord.

There was seen at last, one morning,
  Long months from the first assault,
A speck high up in the azure —
  A bird in the cloudless vault.

The watchers who marked it flying,
  Perceived that it came from sea,

4*

And wondered, as well at its swiftness,
  As what its intent might be.

Until, as it speeded nearer,
  They waited, eager to know
The news from the fleet in North Aa
  And the admiral, good Boisot.

It rose high over the Spaniards,
  And sank, with a gentle flight,
On the shoulder of one who had lingered,
  And watched there all the night.

And this was the message sent them,
  That, soon as the tide would make,
Boisot would slip from his moorings,
  And sail for the inner lake.

Then bells rang out from the steeples,
  Then men kissed men on the street,
Then stern old burghers, like children,
  Climbed up to look for the fleet.

Then toil was forgotten wholly,
  And pain and despair were past,
And days which had fled were as nothing
  To this which should be the last.

But again the gathering blackness
  Swept down and obscured their way;
And, just as it seemed the morning,
  There came no answering ray.

For the waters crept on but slowly,
  As if but to mock their hope;
While steadily fixed in waiting
  Were the troops of the angry Pope.

And William of Orange, faithful
  To them, and to God, and right,
Found the brave Boisot unable
  To sail or commence the fight.

Till, suddenly from the fastness
  Where tempests are wont to hide,
A great wind, full from the ocean,
  Drove up with the rising tide.

And then, borne on by its current
  Through the dikes it had broken down,
Boisot and his tried companions
  Dashed forward to help the town.

In the blackest of the midnight came the challenge of the foe,
And the waters flamed in answer with the cannon's sudden glow,
And amid the sunken houses, and above the sunken plain,
In the thickest of the darkness fell fast the leaden rain.

Still forward pressed the vessels with their fiery Zealand crew,
Bursting down the dikes before them as the wind and tide leaped through;

While the keen eyes of the pilots, through the meshes of the storm,
Caught now and then direction from some well-remembered form.

And the oars pulsed true and grandly, and the waters flaked and flew
In wakes of phosphorescence from the rowing of the crew;
And they saw each others' faces in the cannon's fitful light,
While each prow pierced truly onward like a wedge against the night.

And on they rushed unheeding, shouldered forward now and then,
When they grounded in the shallows, by the muscles of the men;
One gallant purpose guiding, one faith in God and right,
One high and bold endeavor to die or win the fight.

And Leyden watched, all trembling — so strong the feeling ran —
Lest this might prove a conflict too hard for any man.
And Valdez watched, with terror — for the waters deepened fast —
Lest saints, and ground, and army should all desert at last.

All night Boisot fought bravely, and in the early day
He saw the routed Spaniards as they hurried from
his way;
Then full before the fortress, which stayed him last
of all,
He dropped his anchors, resting till the night began
to fall.

And to them who were in the city
Van Werf spoke burning things,
Of the glory of noble daring,
And the victory valor brings.

Till the thin, long hands clutched tighter
Their hold upon sword and pike,
And they waited only his summons
To bid them where to strike.

And the night came down with noises
So full of an awful dread,
That men seemed visibly fighting
With the army of the dead.

For the city wall fell outward,
And crashed with a horrid din,
And the sentinels on the ramparts
Alarmed their friends within.

And lights were seen in the distance
To flicker, now here, now there,
As if ghosts were out in the midnight
And wandered in upper air.

Till the night, so long with its terror,
  Passed on, and the streaks of gray
High over the eastern heaven
  Declared it another day.

And soon it dawned, across the level sweep
Of plains once more surrendered to the deep.
The admiral looked out with eager glance,
Watching his fittest moment to advance.
But all was still — a silence as of death
Left the broad mere without a passing breath.
Amazed, he wondered if an evil fate
Had helped the Spaniards through the city's gate;
And reasoned much, and sickened with the fear
That all had failed when succor was so near.

At last a little boy was seen to stand
Upon the fort and beckon with his hand,
And, wading through the shallow lake, a man
Proclaimed the end of Valdez' haughty plan.
The foe had fled by night, and left no more
Their hated presence on the trampled shore,
And nothing now was needed but to bring
Provision to the starved and famishing.

Again the sailors tore their vessels through
With steady muscles and a stroke as true.
The city gates swung open, and the crowd
Lined the canals, and shouted long and loud.

Then Adrian Van Werf, with hands upraised,
Gave Him the glory, who alone is praised;

And good Boisot, approaching from the fleet,
Headed the great procession up the street.

Fierce Zealanders were there, whose swarthy arms
Were scarred by sword-cuts and with sailor-charms;
Burghers, whose faces, blackened by the fight,
Yet showed their deadly pallor in the light;
Sailors and soldiers, women gaunt and weak,
With hollow eyes and sadly furrowed cheek —
As if their tears, like swollen streams, had worn
Into their souls the sorrow they had borne;
And magistrates commingled with the throng;
And little children tottering along.

These, with a single heart of faith and love,
Entered the church to render thanks to God.
And swelling upward from the thousands there,
Rose one great anthem of their gratitude;
Which, in its rapture, echoed far and near,
Smote the stained windows, proved the fretted work
Through the carved ceiling, and the noble psalm
Bore up all thoughts in wondrous melody.
The deep-toned music thundered down the nave,
Gathering the thankfulness of every soul
Into itself, and swept aloft to God.

And as they sang, and as the organ-notes
Melted on high in waves of harmony,
The overflooded gates of tears gave way.
The music ceased; for this was more than sound
Could ever fathom — deeper than the praise
Which mortal lips can utter.

Only then,
When tongues are loosed, when all our rapture here
Can pass beyond the boundaries of art;
When we shall be transformed to perfectness,
From such imperfect efforts of our lives —
Aye, only then, when faith is lost in sight,
When these poor eyes shall see and fully know
The manifold omniscience which upholds —
Then, only then, with voices tuned of God,
With hands whose skill the angels may not win,
Can we attain to symphonies divine,
And true thanksgiving to our Lord and King.

Until that time, that holy, happy time,
Our loftiest anthems cannot speak our love;
And we, as they, can only bow and cry:
"Our hearts Thou knowest. Take our worthless praise."

And none bent there of all, whose bosom heaved
With such sublime emotion unto God,
As that grand burgher of the Netherlands,
With whom his duty was the guiding-star.
For he had wrestled strongly with himself,
Had beaten down all pride and self-conceit,
Had fought the fight, and now this final day
Had crowned with glory his heroic life.

ON THE WAY.

"Tendimus in Latium." — VIRGIL.

THE blue wave curls about the prow,
  The light breeze ripples o'er the sea,
The clouds sweep gently o'er the brow
  Of fair Trinacrian Sicily;
And yonder lies the yellow sand
Which girds the promised Latian land.

Brave hearts, across the stormy deep
  You held the faith you pledged of old;
For you the gods in waiting, keep
  Rich lands and herds and sunny gold;
For yonder gleams the yellow sand,
Our fated home, the Latian land.

There sterner walls than Troy shall rise,
  And people strong in arms shall dwell,
And, canopied by happy skies,
  For us and ours shall all be well.
Gleam brighter, then, O yellow sand!
Come speedily, O Latian land!

O promised rest! O end of toil!
  O country sought for long in vain!
Soon shall we reach thy favored soil,
  Soon find the guerdon of our pain;
For nearer seems that yellow sand,
And nearer grows the Latian land.

No more shall dread of danger come;
  No more shall threats of storm increase;
Within that sacred, destined home,
  At last, at last we rest in peace,
Beyond the belt of yellow sand,
In that oft-promised Latian land.

WOVEN IN WAR-TIME.

RED, WHITE, AND BLUE.

1862.

WHITE snow upon the field and fold,
Upon the hills, across the wood,
Where the strong oak-leaves long have stood
Against the winter's frost and cold.

Blue sky above them, looking down
Where whitened slopes and meadows lay
With promise of such glorious day
As never tarries with the town.

Red blood of those who fought and fell
To guard our cherished flag from wrong;
Of whom we say, "Their vigil long
Has closed at last, and all is well!"

Blue sky still spreading calmly o'er;
White snow now reddened from the fight,
And one, upon the captured height,
Whose stiffened limbs shall move no more.

THE OLD AND THE NEW SALAMIS.

"Cras ingens iterabimus aequor."

WHO fears when Teucer leads the way?
  Our realms are wider than we know;
And reaching onward through the day,
  Our hope and courage stronger grow.

Who fears? The sea is calm and still;
  Far worse than this we once endured.
O comrades, tried by every ill,
  Why faint when all is just assured?

Old Salamis behind us stands;
  We barred ourselves her open gates;
We took the venture in our hands
  To journey where the future waits.

Not falsely has Apollo said;
  Not falsely came the Delphic voice;
We left the dying with their dead,
  And all the gods approve our choice.

Old Salamis may stand alone;
  Her young, heroic life is here;
Her walls shall crumble stone by stone,
  Her people fail because of fear:

But Salamis on other shores —
  New Salamis, in pride shall rise;
Brave hearts shall guard her through the wars,
  And raise her honor to the skies.

Secure, in prophecy of good,
  We may advance while others fear,
And conquer that which once withstood,
  By faithful sword and trusty spear.

Crown us, O hope of years to be!
  Crown us, whom all the gods shall keep
For, strong because of Liberty,
  We shall attempt the mighty deep.

1865.

ON THE HIGH SEAS.

1865.

How slowly moved these warning years,
  And we as slow to heed their voice;
  Though, while they seemed to say, "Rejoice!"
They left us legacies of tears.

We walked upon the quaking crust
  Above the fiery lava-stream;
  We walked in peace, as in a dream,
Secure and careless in our trust.

We heard beneath our very feet
  The chafing of the burning flow;
  We felt the surging to and fro,
The ceaseless, steady throb and beat.

We knew it not, and yet we trod
  Upon a great imprisoned soul,
  Which strove against unjust control,
Whose agonies were known of God.

Our eyes were dim because of sin,
  Our ears were stopped because of crime,
  Till, in the fulness of His time,
The feeble barrier-crust brake in.

We met the surges face to face,
  Those throbbings which had sapped our strength.

At length we learned our sin — at length
We stood in helpless, mute disgrace.

And then we called aloud on God,
Whose ear had heard the bondman's cry,
Up through whose deep, unfathomed sky
Had pierced the echoes of the rod.

We called on Him, but not aright:
Still in our pride, we bowed not yet;
We reached no depth of true regret;
We struggled blindly in the night.

But at the last there grew a prayer,
Out of our grieving hearts expressed,
For hope in trouble, and for rest
Amid these billows of despair.

He heard us, and we see the day
When, Right is rising over Wrong,
When, from that night, so dark and long,
The clouds are slowly borne away.

He holds the floods within His hand,
He stays the fire's destructive wrath,
And opens us once more a path
Unto a safe and pleasant land.

God help us still! — we ask no more;
For His are all the hearts of men,
And His shall be the glory, when
We reach at last the destined shore.

THE FAITH OF THE HOUR.

1864.

In meekness where we once were proud,
In faith where once our trust was small,
We look beyond the stormy cloud,
And honor Him who gave us all.

For so we learn. The moments teach
Deep things of God, half understood;
And whisper gently, each to each,
Of Law and Right and Brotherhood.

We stand to-day more closely knit
By one great feeling, broad and grand—
That men of every blood are fit
For equal rank in Freedom's land.

All else was easier than this—
To look beneath the husk of things,
To see, below the chrysalis,
The moving of the prisoned wings.

We only held our selfish aims;
We only heard, but did not feel,
When, rising up through godless claims,
Came that unpitied, faint appeal.

Till, guided as we knew not how,
  The scales of blindness fell away,
And, high above the nation, now
  Shines on the dawn of Freedom's day.

For so we purge ourselves from crime;
  And, so, our fathers' joy obtain,
That, through this second troublous time
  Victorious, we shall pass again.

We wait for words of daily cheer;
  And, as they echo through the land,
With purer hearts we cease from fear—
  We know the end is near at hand.

RICHMOND!

APRIL 3d, 1865.

BELL for bell gives answer proudly
  Through the mellow April sun,
Flag for flag waves back a token
  Of the joy for what is done,
For the long, long watch is over,
  And the victory is won.

Let the echoes, then, in triumph
  Ring throughout the country side;
Let the happy greetings beacon
  Over hill and valley wide,
For they stand as conquered foemen —
  They who God and Right defied.

Such the crown He gives to patience
  Who has bid us pray and wait;
Such the glory that He grants us,
  When we triumph over Hate;
Such the promise of the future,
  Through the half-unfolded gate.

"Richmond ours!" We look beyond it,
  To the years which yet shall be;
To the days of peace and plenty —
  To the days when all are free;
To the time when Human Bondage
  Shall be Human Liberty.

Honored be a Higher Wisdom —
  One above has heard our prayer,
One above has marked our sorrow
  Through the battle-clouded air;
One above has been beside us —
  Helped our weakness everywhere.

And to Him this day be glory —
  To His name be songs of praise;
Unto Him be richest blessings
  Which our grateful hearts can raise;
Let Him triumph who has brought us
  To this best of all our days.

For His hand has led us onward
  Underneath the stormy sky,
And in all our darkest moments
  We have fought beneath His eye;
While, with tenderness and mercy,
  He has watched us from on high.

Ring the bell, and swing the banner —
  Let the music rise and swell,
Over hill and valley passing,
  By the brook and through the dell;
Sweep the chorus gladly onward —
  God be praised, for all is well!

A MEMORY.

1866.

SHOULDER to shoulder in serried rank,
  Stern and calm, how the faces run,
As we follow the glint, from flank to flank,
Of musket-barrel and bayonet-shank,
  Under the glow of the setting sun!

Comrade by comrade upon the ground,
  Mown and reaped by the dashing shot,
With a flash of trappings, amid the mound,
From those who suffer without a sound —
  Shiver with anguish, but own it not.

These are the ones who, without regret,
  Gave their lives for their country's cause;
Who are ours as stars in our banner set —
Who died, but whose names are our watchwords
    yet —
  Martyrs for freedom and truth and laws.

DECORATION DAY.

1869.

AFTER the rain when the clouds have broken,
  After the gray when the blue appears,
Trustiest hands have brought a token,
  Sacred because of bloody years.

Whether they sleep in sun or shadow,
  Vanquished by long or sudden pain,
Over their graves on hill and meadow
  Glory of flowers is strewn again.

Under the oak-leaves strong and tender,
  Meshed with the golden threads of light,
Praises arise for each defender,
  Casketed here because of right.

Open, O skies, with swift libation,
  Now that the past is gathered up:
These are the proofs of our probation —
  These who have drained the bitter cup.

Whether they fell in siege or sally,
  Smitten by night or pierced at noon,
Here they have passed within that valley,
  Destined to Death — yet sadly soon!

Seed of the nation's hope and glory,
  Thus have we helped your growth to-day,
Hearing and telling all the story,
  Fairer than gifts which fade away.

What though the harvest dimly beckons
  Out of the promise of the sod,
Faith shall be ours, and care, which reckons
  Love to our land as next to God.

WOVEN FROM CHURCH PATTERNS.

6*

SABRICIUS.

AT Antioch, where first the holy name
Of Christ upon His true disciples came —
Where they were Christians who had learned to live
In higher pleasure than this world can give —
There dwelt two men who, by a common tie,
Were bound to serve the truth and hate the lie.
Not long ago the clouds beneath the blue
Broke wide apart to let the Saviour through;
Not long ago the steadfast eyes of men
Gazed upward after Him who comes again:
Nor were there many years since some could tell
Of Him by whom they saw the sick made well.

The fervor of His pure and perfect word
Yet rang in ears which even, as they heard,
Recalled how like, in all His mighty plan,
Were the instructions of the Son of Man;
How constantly above the surging crowd
That warning voice, with accents clear and loud,

Had cried "Repent!" and bidden all obey
Before the terrors of a final day;
And how, as constantly, that silver tongue
Had charmed the tempers of the old and young,
And cried, "Believe! because the Father's love
Hath sent salvation to you from above!"
And thus these messages were borne along
On sacred lives and on the wings of song.
"Repent!" was written in each holy book;
"Believe!" shone forth in every loving look;
And, simply with this trust before their eyes,
Men left the earth and walked in Paradise.
Before such souls the boundary sky swept back
On either side, and showed a shining track,
And the hard way of daily toil and care
Became the golden street of upper air.

The faith which held such glorious reward
Possessed those watchers for the coming Lord.
They lived sweet lives of innocence and peace;
They saw sin languish and the church increase;
They held themselves unworthy at the best
To wear the garments of a wedding guest,
And, cleaving closer to this central thought,
The praise of Christ above all praise they sought.

Among them, thus abiding in content,
These two were seen, whose willing footsteps went
Day after day where God was found apart
By them of humble and of contrite heart.

The one, Sabricius, at the altar's side
Spake of that Jesus who was crucified.
His words were tender as the tale was told,
Which still is new, nor ever shall grow old;
His hand, as though it held a flaming sword,
Defied the persecutors of his Lord;
He stood like Peter, seeming to declare,
"Where'er thou goest, thou shalt find *me* there."
Albeit some, whose heads were snowy white,
Said, "They that threaten do not always fight."
And ofttimes solemnly were heard to say,
"It was not thus in the Apostles' day."

The other was Nicephorus — a man
Benignant, and in whom all virtues ran
Like streams together, fresh and full and strong —
Rivers of God serenely borne along.
No priest was he — no waiting ears drank in
His splendid sentences concerning sin;
No neophyte, with sympathetic trust,
Craved benediction, kneeling in the dust;
No glory of a sacerdotal state
Had made him distant, cold, and separate;
He only strove, with many prayers and tears,
To win approval for his earthly years.

They met in duties of their daily lot,
And, most of all, in some secluded spot
Where poor, faint voices clamored after bread,
Or where they raised some dying sinner's head,

That he might see by faith an open gate,
And enter in before it grew too late.
Thus meeting, both with mutual esteem
Beheld each other through a common theme;
Yet did Sabricius now and then disclose
The presence in him of our fiercest foes:
Pride, and the love of self, and even more
Trampled across his heart and bruised it sore;
And, save for duties of his priestly place,
The homes of sadness had not seen his face.
But yet his spirit took a strange delight
In holding him severely to the right,
And never, though his soul was greatly stirred,
Were these his inward tumults overheard.

Not so Nicephorus. For him no rule
Of fear was known within the Saviour's school;
Love kept his goings out and comings in;
Love shielded him from the assaults of sin;
Love sent him to the hungry and the faint;
Love bade him help the much-encumbered saint;
And, wheresoever any priests had call,
They found Nicephorus before them all.
Some angel of the Lord with speech divine
Had doubtless helped him by a secret sign—
For what are these our instincts to do good,
Save thoughts, which in the Father's presence stood?

The years passed onward. They of whom I speak
Were faithful still to all the worn and weak;

Until at last — I know not why or how —
There came a cloud upon Sabricius' brow:
Nicephorus aggrieved him — how or why,
The elder chroniclers know more than I.
Sufficient is it that the sword of wrath
Clove, as it always does, a sudden path;
And they, whose prayers had often risen up
With arms entwined — for whom a single cup
Held the red wine of sacramental joy —
Whose feet were foremost in the same employ —
Went divers ways, and all the church beheld
One of those scandals which are seldom quelled.

Then once again upon the Christians came
That devil's vengeance of the sword and flame.
The woodman Death, delighted with his toil,
Hewed God's good trees quite level with the soil.
The church lost heart, as here and there it saw
Another victim of Valerian's law;
For he was emperor, and day by day
He broke the stoutest of the saints away.

Sabricius still, as yet unpacified,
Left patience, favor, pardon — all denied.
He spurned Nicephorus so much the more
As he sought entrance at the bolted door.
He would not hear nor heed that holy man,
Seeking forgiveness as the day began;
He would not see nor save that patient one,
Seeking forgiveness with the setting sun.

He hardened through the precepts of a creed
Wherein he often taught himself to read
The Gospel as the Law, and where, instead
Of "giving to thine enemy his bread,"
He saw enrolled, in ragged, lightning lines,
The harsh, sad justice of the ancient signs,
That "eye for eye and tooth for tooth must pay,
And he be stoned who would not thus obey."
No persecution stayed his burning zeal,
Or closed his lips from warning and appeal.
He rather loved, with look and speech austere,
To cry aloud in that most awful year.
Nor did it seem to any who observed
His steady valor that he ever swerved
From right and truth and peace, and thus at last
A tacit verdict favorably passed:
And good Nicephorus, on either side
Beset, and with all pardon still denied,
Went broken-hearted where a few remained
Who could not fancy that his soul was stained.

The persecution burned with keener light
Amid the gloom of spiritual night;
And now, while serving at the altar's side,
They seized Sabricius, full of priestly pride.
Indignantly he treated any thought
That piety so perfect could be bought.
He called their idols blocks of wood and stone;
Their emperor, a pigmy on a throne;
Their laws, the breath of hell; their threats and rage,
The rant of actors on a creaking stage.

All this and more he shouted for the throng
To understand, as he was dragged along.

Thus speaking in the haughtiness of pride,
He turned and saw the swaying crowd divide,
And, pressing through, Nicephorus draw near
Unhesitating and without a fear.
Once more he pleaded for forgiving grace
Before they reached that last and dreadful place,
Where Roman fagots, or the Roman sword,
Would send the martyr to his martyred Lord;
And once again, with hard and bitter speech,
Was met by doctrines which the Rabbis teach.
But for that one whose prayers and tears in vain
Besought the favor which they ought to gain
Not even this sufficed, and still he came
Close after him with penitence and shame.
The people followed, hearing now and then
This strangest conference of Christian men,
Until it ceased, because they both could see
That on that spot the end of earth must be.

Then swiftly, from the post they held so well,
Sabricius' pride and haughty temper fell.
His fear, as though in very pangs of death,
Caught at his heart, and stopped his steady breath.
He glared, grew white, and, smitten with dismay,
Was ready next to sell his soul, and say
That Jove was greater than Jehovah, or
That He was but a man whom Mary bore.

Amazed, Nicephorus again besought
The failing priest to battle as he ought;
But still, alas! in vain; for sudden dread
Had left him spiritless and nearly dead.
Wherefore with speed he turned himself about,
Erect and calm, delivered from his doubt,
And bade the prefect *take him in the stead*
Of this his enemy, and, smiling, said,
"Perhaps our God, if he shall longer live,
Will grant forgiveness as I now forgive;
And he who spurned the sinner from his side
May gain that pardon which he once denied."

A moment more, and then a martyr's crown
Was on the head which bowed so bravely down;
A moment more, and that hard heart of years
Had broken forth in true and humble tears;
A moment more, and then there went away
One who took hold on Christ and learned to pray.

LAURENTIUS.

THIS is the story which is told
Of the Church of Christ in days of old,
Before its purpose was warped and bent
Out of its first and best intent.
This is the legend, strange and true,
Of one who did what he found to do.

In Decius' time, when o'er the land
The persecuting flame was fanned,
The good Laurentius, of Rome,
Abode in peacefulness at home.
The care was his, each Sabbath day,
To bear the church's gifts away,
And, through the coming week, secure
These benefactions to the poor.
Daily he gave, and ever fed
The hungry with their daily bread;
And those whom others had denied
His Christian charity supplied.
He raised no mansion to allure
The thronging myriads of poor;
But to the prefect one had showed
What blessings from his bounty flowed.
How freely, yet how fairly, fell
Those heavenly guerdons none may tell
Until, with those who walk with God,
The footsteps of our faith have trod.

But now the emperor's decree
Went forth and traversed Italy,
That there should be the strictest search
To gather money from the Church;
And, through the deacons, to extort
Whatever might adorn the court.
Prætor and ædile then began
With speed to carry out the plan;
And robbing thus, of course retained
Their portion of the plunder gained.

Most of all else one prefect's eye
Was loth to pass Laurentius by;
Not any deacon seemed more free
In charitable works than he.
To seize the hoard from which he spent
Was surely what his lord had meant.
Honor and wealth and all the band
Of high preferments were at hand,
If only one might prove his zeal
As prompt to plan and apt to steal.

He caught the deacon unawares,
Returning from the evening prayers,
And harshly, with a look and frown
Designed to beat resistance down,
"Show me," he cried, "your church's gold;
For you possess it, I am told."

The meek Laurentius, with eyes
Bright in the gleams of Paradise,

And wrinkled face, through which there ran
A glory undiscerned of man,
Looked up and smiled, and seemed to be
A monarch in his majesty.
He quivered not with any dread,
Nor bowed at all his snowy head,
But stood serene and calm and grand
Before those words of stern command.
His threadbare mantle, flowing down,
Was graceful as a consul's gown;
And, though no purple stripe it bore,
Displayed its owner's worth the more.
Silent he stood before the throng,
Weak in his age, yet proudly strong,
And raised his voice in mild reply:
"Give me three days in which to try
And redemand from every source
Our sacred treasure without force.
Many are those to whom I go;
Much has been loaned, and much we owe."

The greedy prefect, glad at heart
Since fate made this the better art,
Unhesitating, granted grace
For such delay and such a space
Of time before his hopes of gold
Should grow and blossom manifold.

The days of respite passed, and then
Laurentius appeared again

And gave him this inviting word:
"Come, see the treasure of our Lord!
A court in which you shall behold
Uncounted vessels, all of gold;
And porches never heaped before
With such a wealth of shining ore."

The prefect rubbed his hands in glee,
And followed him with ecstasy,
As one who, watching far and wide
The footprints of the falling tide,
Discerns some rare and perfect pearl
Cast upward by the ocean's whirl.
Street after street he followed through
In haste the promised sight to view,
And ever came the eager thought
That even quaestorships were bought.

At last, through portals high and fair,
They reached the Christians' place of prayer,
And, crowding in the court around,
A multitude possessed the ground.
The prefect looked, and, in amaze,
Continued still his earnest gaze;
For still, on every side, he saw
The victims of a cruel law:
Beggars, in rank and in degree
The very lords of beggary;
The crippled hero of the wars,
In all his panoply of scars;

The gladiator, gashed and torn
By lion's claws or bison's horn;
The slave, his brawny shoulders bare,
Latticed with scourgings everywhere;
The strange and terrible array
Of those who must be always gay,
Who strive forever to beguile
With fixed and artificial smile —
Flute-girls and dancers, whom their fate
Had made the playthings of the great;
The foam and frothing on the brink
Of bitterness which Rome should drink.

All these and other sights of pain
Were seen, and yet were seen in vain;
For other, sadder shapes of woe,
Before his eyes made haste to go.
And, miserable in the shade
Which the extended porches made,
Lay those, worn out with old disease,
Whose cup of life was at its lees;
The lame, the maimed, the weak, the blind,
Were they who thus remained behind.

In doubt as yet what this might mean,
The prefect paused, and stood between
Two marble pillars, much perplexed,
Fearing the mob and sorely vexed.

"Behold!" once more Laurentius said,
"The bequests of our sainted dead.

These are our treasures, better far
Than gold and gems and silver are.
These are crown-jewels of the bride
Which make her fit for Jesus' side.
Take them for him who sent you here,
And use them in the Master's fear.
Take them for Rome; and take them, too,
As better wealth than you pursue;
For he who giveth to the Lord
Shall never lose his sure reward."

Abashed, the prefect turned away.
But further none can truly say,
Since only in God's judgment-book
Is scrolled what future course he took.

TEXTUS RECEPTUS.

The Brother Anselmus, in his cell
Scrolled the New Testament wondrous well.

Letter by letter across the page
Crept on the marvellous heritage.

Before each chapter he treasured space
For a rare device or an angel's face.

With gold and azure and crimson lines
He traced the shape of his quaint designs.

Initial-letters, once rude and bare,
Under his tinting grew warm and fair;

And flowers of the choicest twined and clung
Where vines depended and branches swung.

Amid a desert of blackest text
They succored the mind of one perplexed;

Making oases in which to pause
And meditate upon holy laws.

For Brother Anselmus, morn by morn,
Saw better visions of beauty born;

And over his labors, night by night,
Sat reasoning in a calm delight:

Until it passed to a cloister jest,
That with him to work was to be at rest.

But many scoffed when they did not see
A fitting end to his mystery;

And some asserted, as friars do,
That Brother Anselmus was not true;

For he spent his efforts, as they averred,
On other work than the Blessèd Word —

A deed of guilt, since it dared withstand
Their abbot's saintliest reprimand.

Thus they who cavilled and he who toiled
Apart, in their daily lives recoiled.

Yet the lonely monk at his ancient desk
Wove in black letter with arabesque.

Gospels of Matthew and Mark and Luke
Were far in the front of his vellum book.

And then, succeeding to these, went on
The precious record of loving John,

The Acts and Epistles manifold
Of saints, whose titles were wrought in gold.

At last his pen, with a careful touch,
Delayed at the name he loved so much —

Entering truly and well upon
The First Epistle of dear Saint John.

Its glorious message of comfort brought
That peace which Anselmus long had sought;

And he traced the lines with a tender care
For thoughts of joy which were hidden there.

Initial-letter and chapter-head
Were never bedaubed with heedless red;

But lovingly, and with patient art,
Became the history of his heart:

As if he wrote for the world indeed
That story of faith which God can read.

And once, late on in the winter gloom,
When his lamp but feebly lit the room,

He saw, in the focus of its rays,
A sentence fashioned of trust and praise—

That "whatsoever of God is born
Overcometh all earthly scorn,"

And "this, our faith, is the victory
Which overcometh its enmity."

The Brother Anselmus laid his quill
Quietly down, and pondered still:

And then, with a heart relieved from doubt,
He scrolled it in golden ink throughout:

And none but the angels floating by
Had caught the sound of his final sigh.

But they found him at matins still and cold,
His dead lips touching the text of gold.

And when they bore him away to rest,
They placed his volume upon his breast,

Clasping his hands above the word
For which he listened—and which he heard.

CHRISTMAS-TIME, 1866.

CYPRIAN'S WORDS.

SPAKE good Cyprian of Carthage well and wisely, once of old,
Writing down his own heart-teaching as in manuscript of gold:

"God would have us tried and sifted, and the hearts that still believe,
Strength and help in all affliction, from the Father shall receive."

Years ago that bishop holy left the Mauritanian shore,
Tried indeed with all affliction, martyred for the faith he bore;

But his words, to-day as precious as they were in other days,
Bear about them in his honor better far than earthly praise.

Fainting in our feeble efforts, failing in our meagre faith,
Well may we in shame and sorrow ponder what the martyr saith.

So, from trust approved in trial, we may learn a higher life;
So, from bitter persecution, learn to bear this lesser strife.

All the day shall not be darkness, all the night shall
not be pain;
And though years may pass but slowly, we shall
reach to light again.

THE PICTURE OF CHRIST.

UNDER the gathered dust of years
Many a time the truth appears;
Many a time the words of old
Shine the better when freshly told;
And over their story hangs a praise
Growing nobler by lapse of days.
Such are the tales of early date
Concerning bishop and celibate,
Concerning wonders the martyrs wrought,
Concerning treasures the churches brought,
Concerning much now long left out,
Which quaint Baronius wrote about.

His are the folios, dark with age,
Wherein are annals of seer and sage,
Printed when Faust's inventive hand
Not long had lifted the glowing brand
Of that pure fire of a knowledge freed
From harsh dominion and selfish creed.
Here, on the page of each bulky tome
A black-art mystery seems at home.
Here, in such Latin as classics hate,
Is record of Constantine the Great.
The marvellous history here unrolls
Of sainted heroes with holy souls,
Of Peter and Paul and divers others,
Bishops and deacons and lay-brothers;

Of women, mighty in all good deeds,
And "ladies elect" in widow's weeds;
Of Nero's circus, when games began
Where each blazing torch was a living man;
Of caves which ramify under Rome,
Where the threatened Christians found a home,
Holding a church in a catacomb.

These, and the like, each student still
Can read and ponder as he will:
Yet one old legend may be spared,
Culled from a myriad undeclared.

Here followeth then, in modern phrase,
Baronius' story of ancient days.

Constantia, sister of Constantine,
Was given to thought of things divine.
Sylvester had laid upon her head
Baptismal blessing before she wed,
And thus at Rome, in the holy place,
She followed the fashion of her race,
Owning herself by the bishop's hands
No longer subject to Satan's bands.

Her husband, Caius Licinius,
While in the East, grew mutinous,
And, fighting against his rightful liege
At Nicomedia, lost the siege;
Ending at last a conquered lord,
And dying under the headsman's sword.

She then, a widow, dwelt peacefully,
And wished to pray in obscurity,
Quietly waiting for the day
When mortal troubles shall pass away.
Yet was her fate of another sort.
Her brother replaced her in his court,
And there, beset upon every side
With words of praise and with thoughts of pride,
Her life shone out like a splendid star,
And cast its lustre serene and far.

At Nicomedia dwelt a man —
Eusebius, the historian —
Who, in his volume, says that he
Has seen the Christ of Calvary.
Not in his human shape alone —
For three whole centuries then had flown;
But still in image as rarely true
As any mortal might dare to view; —
He saw St. Paul and St. Peter too —
And these were portraits, preserved with care,
Whose tone and tinting were wondrous fair.

Him had Constantia questioned much
Of these sweet relics and other such;
And he, as Bishop of Palestine,
Told her about that One divine —
Yet said no more to describe the face
Than here I say in this later place.
Of Peter and Paul he talked with ease,
And spoke of the famed symbolic keys.

He mentioned the painter's skill and art,
The feeling of truth in every part,
The certainty which his mind received
That these were faces to be believed.
But always he stopped most reverently
At the last description of the three
Not telling his vision openly.

Constantia often longed in vain
To cause the bishop to be more plain;
And finally, after years of thought,
Grew wholly bent upon what she sought.
The Christ of Calvary, raised on high —
Ascending, never again to die —
Had left behind Him this holy trace,
This one true likeness, this perfect face.
And if, by means which were still untried,
She too might see it before she died,
This would repay her waiting years,
Her faithful vigils and prayerful tears.

To Nicomedia then she went
On such an errand of pure intent,
But finding Eusebius far from thence,
Active in all benevolence,
And busied with matters of the Church,
She wrote him letters about her search:
"Where could this face of Christ be found?
In what abode of the region round?
Who was its guardian? Who possessed

This treasure, rarer than all the rest?
Where was its crypt, or cave, or chest?
Let him send it, that she might view
That very Christ the Apostles knew."

Again and again did words like these
Follow him over his diocese,
Until, as she would not be denied,
The Bishop Eusebius replied.

"You wish," he writes, "that myself should send
The image of Christ to you, my friend;
But tell me fairly and candidly
What do you think that this may be?
Is it that one, unchanged and true,
Which has no age and is ever new,
Which bore our nature yet kept its own,
And which is the right of God alone?
With this, I trust, you are not concerned,
Since you, from the Scriptures having learned,
Cannot mistake the Apostle's speech,
'That none may ever the knowledge reach
Of God the Father, save God the Son;
Nor can there be found a single one
To know the Son save the Father only.'
In short, that here is an image lonely;
Which none may touch, and which none attain,
So long as sin and ourselves remain.

"Nor do I think that image meant
Where God and man, in one person blent,

Trod the stained earth with His sinless feet,
Felt in His bosom our sorrows beat,
Bore in Himself our human fears,
Wept over us such godlike tears,
Died for our sake such a human death,
Rose for our sake with such godlike breath —
That truly these are so woven in,
The sinful with that which cannot sin,
The human with that which is all divine,
As no mere mortal can well define.
Who, therefore, by colors so dead and cold
Can show the splendor which shone of old,
Can paint the God and the man — that face
In its mortal and yet immortal grace?
Who, by a picture transitory,
Can tell one half of the holy story?
For they who loved him the first and chief —
Who held to Him with the best belief —
When on the mountain apart from men,
Saw Him too wondrous for tongue or pen,
And, falling prone at the awful sight,
Could not endure so great a light!

"If, then, His figure when here on earth
Received such power from His sacred birth;
If this dear Saviour could not be known
When here apart from the Father's throne —
What must it be when now He reigns
Above the torment of human pains?
No painted image can reach Him there,
No artist's pencil His face declare.

"I do not send you the likeness, then.
Far better than this may be yours: for when
You search your heart as you search the land,
And plan with zeal as you now have planned;
When thought goes out to all holy things;
When your soul has eyes, and your prayers have
wings;
When the hardest toil of our common lot
Becomes transformed, and its pain is not;
When penitence for the sinful life
Welds the armor for nobler strife —
Then, at last, you are near your goal,
For the face of the Lord is upon your soul,
And faith, in your faithful life can see
The image of Christ of Calvary."

And here Baronius turns the page,
And adds long records of saint and sage.
The old black-letter runs on again
Like a turbid stream after summer rain.
But I close the book, for its tale is told —
That story new, though it seemeth old;
And I sit in silence, since here indeed
The dead have written for me to read.

WOVEN AT ODD HOURS.

THE TYRANT OF TROPPAU.

1866.

IN the foreign war which is ended now,
It happened (I cannot tell you how)
That the Prussian infantry held Troppau.
One poor sentry was posted there,
At the very top of the steeple stair,
Who, keeping watch upon things without,
Discovered his regiment all in rout,
Hurrying past at their quickest rate,
(Which, in fact, was rather a speedy gait,)
As though they did n't intend to wait:
And then he thought that his time was come
Like them to follow the fife and drum;
And so descended each crooked flight
Of ladders which threaded the dizzy height,
With his musket slung by its leathern strap,
And a century's cobwebs on his cap.
Dirty and breathless he reached the street —
But those were gone whom he hoped to meet.

Was there ever a scrape like this,
Or ever a quandary such as his?

The Prussian backs were a mile away,
And the enemy's army had won the day;
The town was empty of every face
Which seemed to promise him any grace;
So now that he dared not trust the people,
He climbed the stair which was in the steeple,
And there awaited, like any German,
The first assault of the burgher vermin.

He filled his pipe and began to smoke,
Regarding the whole as a kind of joke,
Which might, indeed, be very unpleasant
To some poor, ignorant, helpless peasant,
But not to him of the Prussian corps—
He had heard of such doings long before.
The way, you know, is to keep your wits,
Guard the approaches, and give 'em fits;
Haul up your ladders and stay above,
Ready either to shoot or shove;
Club your musket and rattle down
Blows by the dozen on every crown;
Or settle them all with a steady dose
Of leaden pills administered close:
And thus, if your cartridges only last,
You'll not be captured so very fast.

After a while the citizens came,
Parleyed, palavered, and asked his name,
Wished to know if he would n't come down,
Under their escort, and see the town?

Tried to tempt him in divers ways;
Wearied him much with threats and praise;
Rushed at him up the steeple-stair:
But found that victory was n't there.

How he tumbled the burghers down
Toward the dirt of their ancient town;
How he cunningly saved his powder
While the baffled enemy shouted louder;
How he finally drove them back,
Hammering some like a bruiser's sack —
These are matters which you will find
In the record of him who was left behind.

Well, they ordered him down once more,
Then retreated, and locked the door,
Telling him, in the fiercest way,
To stay and starve, if he wished to stay;
And adding, in grim and ghastly tones,
That some day, doubtless, they 'd find his bones
Lying white on the belfry stones.

To which he answered that it was well
To tell him all that they had to tell;
But as for him, he had ammunition —
Plenty too — and a good position,
And just so sure as they blocked him in,
They would learn that numbers don't always win;
While as to starving, the case was clear:
Their principal street was much too near,

And none should pass till the town agreed
To furnish him with the best of feed!
In short, he proposed to stop their driving,
Unless they would keep him well and thriving.

Quite audacious, as matters stood;
But quite successful, and so as good
As any stratagem, proved and fine,
By which distinguished commanders shine.

The citizens did as he told them to:
There was really nothing else to do;
For who would wish to destroy the trade
By which his *kreuzers* were daily made,
When his only chances of quiet selling
Were during the intervals of shelling?

For two whole days they supplied his need
With fresh provisions, as was agreed.
Silly fellows! they did n't think
Of puttting anything into his drink;
Or stuffing an arsenic-pill within
Some great ham-sausage's smoky skin;
Or giving him plenty of *Schweitzer-kase*,
(In which the skippers run fifty ways;)
Or vitriolizing his *sauer-kraut*
On purpose to try and serve him out;
Or cracking his teeth with the blackest bread
Baked in oven since Noah wed,
And which, as a specimen rare and good,
Came in the ark from before the flood;

Or filling his pipe with a deadly lot
Of *knaster*, destructive as canister-shot;
Or letting him have what was vastly meaner —
A bit from a pig which had died of *trichina*.

They never thought of things like these,
Of bony herring or fatal cheese;
Of *cholera morbus*, induced by means
Of any indigestible greens;
Or a nice brain-fever, produced at pleasure
By heavy philosophers read at leisure —
But simply sent, in their simple way,
The tribute the Prussian made them pay.

Thus he lived on the fat of the land,
Holding Troppau at his own command —
An autocrat, from a steeple's top
Ready to let his lightnings drop,
(As Jove, in the old mythology,
Hurls his thunderbolts down the sky) —
Until his regiment came again
And took the city by might and main:
For then, recruited by steeple-habits,
By *pâtes-de-foix-gras* and stewed rabbits —
By all that the aldermen were able
To spread for the comfort of his table —
He came to meet them, as round and fair
As when he ascended the belfry stair,
And, feeling the benefit of haste,
Invited his comrades in to taste
His beer, that it should not go to waste!

SIR KAY'S EXCUSE.

A CHAPTER FROM THE "MORTE D'ARTHUR."

KING MARKE of Cornwall, on a quiet noon,
When May was passing into leafy June,
Sat by his chamber window at the chess,
And moved the men to cure his idleness;
While all the air around his balcony
Was full and overflowed with melody.
The very birds were fit to rend their throats
In quaint concordance of their rarest notes;
The strong young leaves which wove above his head
Mellowed the glory which the sunlight shed;
The hounds lay sleeping in the court below,
Where the old warder strung a faithful bow;
The hawk upon his perch beside the wall
Ruffled his feathers at a distant call,
But smoothed them soon; the horses near at hand
Found their long respite hard to understand;
For never had a single trumpet's bray
Broken the stillness of that perfect day.
Yet, had King Marke the Cruel been aware
Of what was purposed by Ysolde the Fair,
He had not sat, with features grave and sage,
Playing at chess against his little page.
He would, in truth, have borne the story ill
Of how Sir Tristram had escaped his will;
And much I fear that luckless page had found
Himself as well as chessmen thrust around.

For kings, who have their way, as all must know,
Display their anger often by a blow.
Still, unsuspicious of a coming fate,
King Marke played on with countenance sedate.

Within the turret, just above the trees,
Sir Tristram and Sir Kay abode at ease.
Dame Bragwaine and the fair Ysolde alone
Preserved the secret of this room of stone;
And that dull warden, who perchance could guess
How knights had entered clad in yeomen's dress.
So on this day they watched the king beneath
Tapping upon his jewelled dagger-sheath;
Pushing a bishop to an adverse square,
And taking back his move with crafty care;
Or else, with knitted brow and lip compressed,
Pondering whether this or that were best.
They saw the page, intent upon the game,
Yawn suddenly and dread an open shame—
Concealing with the plume upon his cap
As best he could this unforeseen mishap.
And then Sir Tristram and the mild Sir Kay
Choked with their laughter, even as they lay
Half out of window, peering through the leaves,
And so drew back more guiltily than thieves.
Then, while in merry mood upon the floor
They sat and talked, there entered at the door
Ysolde the Queen, the fairest lady known
Within a cottage or before a throne;
Whose bright, sweet presence caused the room to shine
As though it held some radiant gem divine.

Even for her sake had Kay and Tristram stayed
A fortnight in this nook which she had made;
The while King Marke, with evil in his soul,
Scoured the whole land of which he had control;
And longed to slay Sir Tristram how he would,
But found no happy moment when he could.
They rose upon their feet, and, as they did,
Dropped from Kay's bosom letters which were hid —
Disclosing to Sir Tristram's startled sight
Ysolde's own writing on the crumpled white.
With one quick grasp he snatched them both away
And charged his baseness on the gentle Kay;
While Fair Ysolde, whose pity wrought it all,
Fell in a swoon against the nearest wall;
For though she loved Sir Tristram first and best,
She had been sad to see Sir Kay distressed,
And, as a tender woman might, she sent
No other words than those for friendship meant.

But Tristram, careless of all else beside,
Called on Sir Kay "to guard him, or he died;"
And, rushing on him while his rage was hot,
In one short second all his love forgot.
And Kay, beholding death thus soon and near,
Was strangely smitten so with grief and fear,
That through the opened sash he gave a spring,
And vaulted down upon the heedless king.

The branches crashed, the table broke in twain,
The chessmen scattered, nor were found again;
The page ran howling down the turret stair
Into the chapel, and began a prayer;

The hawk screamed loudly, shaking all his bells;
The hounds bayed answer to the page's yells;
The horses neighed and snorted as they stood;
The warden cursed the noisy neighborhood;
And Kay the Mild, bewildered by his fall,
Stared on each side, nor feared King Marke at all.

Then spoke the king, with his most awful frown,
"Who are you, fellow, that come hurling down
Out of that window, nearly on my head?"
"My lord the king," Sir Kay the Gentle said,
"It fortuned me that in that window-seat
I was asleep, whereby the summer heat
Caused me to slumber sounder than I use,
And so I fell — and this is my excuse."
Then shouted stern King Marke without debate,
"Kick me this fellow through the castle gate!"

That night Sir Tristram, while men's sleep was young,
Reached the great hall where weapons had been hung,
Got him equipment, and by dawn of day,
Was far beyond those portals on his way.

SUMMER READING.

I AM looking through the pages of forgotten old
romances,
Idly thinking, as I read them, of the times now
passed away;
While the bees are in the blossoms, and the mellow
sunshine glances,
And the birds are singing carols all the long, long
summer day.

I am wearing out the moments by a dip into Bonomi,
And the cuneiform inscriptions are puzzling my
poor brain;
So, in sheer despair at trying, I have voted them
below me,
And have bent my whole attention on Monseigneur
de Montaigne.

With his quaint discourse enchanted, I have wan-
dered through the ages,
And have just exchanged his volume for my good
Sir Thomas Browne,
Who has led me, by his quoting from the grand old
Latin sages,
Till, to satisfy my conscience, I have taken Haw-
thorne down.

And, with all the little children who have heard
those tales repeated,
I renew my ancient friendship for the myths of
olden time;
While I only just remember I am at my window
seated,
And am not in distant regions of a mellow Eastern
clime.

Till, recalled by some suggestion of the page which
lies before me,
The features, more familiar, of a nearer friend
arise;
And the spell that holds my fancy, as again it passes
o'er me,
Brings back the quiet welcome of those unforgotten
eyes.

So I lay the book beside me; I am ended for the
morning,
With its words of strange enchantment, for their
power has passed away;
I can think of nothing further than the face that
wears no scorning:
I must read unwritten volumes if I read again
to-day.

SMOKE AND CHESS.

We were sitting at chess as the sun went down,
And he, from his meerschaum's glossy brown,
With a ring of smoke made his king a crown.

The cherry stem, with its amber tip,
Thoughtfully rested on his lip,
As the goblet's rim from which heroes sip.

And, looking out through the early green,
He called on his patron saint, I ween —
That misty maiden, Saint Nicotine;

While ever rested that crown so fair,
Poised in the warm and pulseless air,
On the carven chessman's ivory hair.

Dreamily wandered the game along,
Quietly moving at even-song,
While the striving kings stood firm and strong;

Until that one which of late was crowned
Flinched from a knight's determined bound,
And in sullen majesty left the ground,

Reeling back; and it came to pass
That, waiting to mutter no funeral mass,
A bishop had dealt him the *coup de grace.*

And so, as we sat, we reasoned still
Of fate and of fortune, of human will,
And what are the purposes men fulfil.

For we see at last when the truth arrives
The moves on the chess-board of our lives —
That fields may be lost though the king survives.

Not always he whom the world reveres
Merits its honor or wins its cheers,
Standing the best at the end of years.

Not always he who has lost the fight
Rises again with the coming light,
Battles anew for his ancient right.

A SMALL WARBLER.

A LITTLE bird with the blackest eyes
  Sits on a twig and nods at me;
  Very merry he seems to be,
    And wise.

I wish I knew what the fellow thinks,
  Saucily shaking his cunning head —
  Whether it cannot all be said
    By winks.

I wish I were of the craft as well,
  Careless of morrows which come too soon,
  Hearing the tales a golden noon
    Can tell.

For I should tarry among the leaves,
  Breathing no other than balmy air,
  Seeing my harvest everywhere
    In sheaves.

And then I should tax my brain no more,
  Thick though the snowflakes chose to fall,
  Knowing I have beyond them all
    A shore.

UNDERGRADUATE ORIOLES.

On a picture by Mrs. Emma Seligman, Philadelphia, March 5th, 1867.

FOUR little mouths agape forever;
Four little throats which are never full;
Four little nestlings, who dissever
One big worm by a mighty pull.

Up on a limb — the lazy fellow! —
Perches the father, bold and gay;
Proud of his coat of black and yellow,
Always singing throughout the day.

Close at their side the watchful mother,
Quietly sober in dress and song,
Chooses her place, and asks no other,
Flying and gleaning all day long.

Four little mouths in time grow smaller;
Four little throats in time are filled;
Four little nestlings quite appal her,
Spreading their wings for the sun to gild.

Lazy no longer sits the father;
His is the care of the singing-school:
He must teach them to fly and gather
Splendid worms by the nearest pool.

Swinging away on the shaken branches,
Under the light of the happy sun;
Dropping through blossoms like avalanches—
Father Oriole's work is done.

Four little beaks their mouths embolden;
Four little throats are round and strong;
Four little nestlings, fledged and golden,
Graduate in the world of song.

RENOVATION.

THERE are sounds across the prairie,
Songs of birds which, clear and airy,
        Greet the light;
With the freshening of the clover,
And the wild geese flying over
        All the night.

There are buds of promise starting,
Now that winter is departing,
        And the spring,
Warm and joyous, is returning,
Glowing bright, and, in her yearning,
        Blossoming.

In my heart the spring is coming,
And the insects' distant humming
        Brings again
All the days of mirth and laughter,
As the sunshine follows after
        Early rain.

And the love, long kept and cherished,
Kept, when other loves have perished,
        Buds anew;
Hidden but to prove its fitness,
Rising thus again to witness
        It is true.

ON MY BACK.

Here in the shade amid the clover,
  You shall discover me, friend of mine;
Oak leaf and maple bending over,
  Tangled with tendrils of the vine.

This is my fortress—here I battle
  Evil which grows from the city's thought;
Here I forget the ceaseless rattle,
  Hurry, and toil, which men have wrought.

These are the pages which the summer—
  Diligent student!—thumbs and turns,
Reading in haste, like some late comer,
  Into whose soul the wisdom burns.

Come to me, then. No poet's measure
  Holds to the full this golden day,
Rich in what gifts of countless treasure
  Winter, the miser, hid away.

Hark! to his wife the thrush is calling;
  All the blue sky is thrilled with song;
Now and then through the tree-tops falling,
  Full of a mirth most glad and strong.

Here to the shade amid the clover
  Come, and discover me, friend of mine;
Oak leaf and maple bending over,
  Tangled with tendrils of the vine.

MIDAS.

TREACHEROUS rushes were they that told
The secret won from the barber's fears,
How, spite of kingdom, in spite of gold,
In spite of lineage fair and old,
The great King Midas had asses' ears.

Well, you may doubt that the tale was true,
Quibble and query as much as you will;
And yet, whatever the Greeks might do,
The story has fitness for them and you,
And the truth of its moral is useful still.

For this you may notice, wherever you go,
That each, impelled by his private fears,
Has that which he tells to but one or so—
Some flaw in life to be whispered low—
In short, that each Midas has asses' ears.

Truly hapless, alas! are we
Who think all matters in truth are done:
We wag on our little way in glee,
While we and our Dead-Sea apples agree;
And *then*—naught but lies is beneath the sun.

And the rushes grow up in the hole to-day,
Dreamily murmuring unto the breeze
The secrets men would have hid alway,
Hoping, but failing, by prisons of clay,
To hinder their going wherever they please.

CASTLES IN THE AIR.

I HAVE a palace
Beyond the valleys
Which greet Olympus in Grecian lands;
A misty mansion,
Whose vague expansion
The morning holds in her sunny hands.

Some frozen region
Of realms Norwegian,
With rugged splendors of cape and cliff,
Holds fiords of wonder
Which cleave asunder
Before the bows of my rapid skiff.

My visions vanish
To countries Spanish,
Beneath the glow of Castilian skies;
For there, enchanted,
I dwell, unhaunted
By any terror of prying eyes.

The wildest stories
Of tropic glories
Have failed to utter the truth to me
Of verdant highlands
And fairest islands
Which I possess in the central sea.

Ah, me! no mortal
Can hew the portal
Of solid granite or carven stone;
Nor can I ever,
By long endeavor,
Make these possessions my very own.

The sun each morning
Is freshly scorning
My palace, fashioned of flying clouds;
And northern summers
Find other comers
Than my swift bark with her taughtened shrouds.

My Spanish fastness,
For all its vastness,
Dissolves itself in a golden haze;
And tropic splendor
(That witch of Endor!)
Calls up the ghosts of my buried days.

And thus they leave me,
As some deceive me
In whom I trusted above the rest;
They roll together
Like April weather,
And so pass over beyond the West.

But still I'm building
In Dream-land, gilding

My latest turrets with scattered rays;
And still I 'm sowing
For harvests growing
To full completion in future ways.

In pure fee-simple
Each sunny dimple,
Each fresh, bright land of the earth is mine;
And each new season
But adds a reason
To sanction me in my right divine.

O homes unreckoned!
Whose pleasures beckoned
Throughout the modes of my changing dream,
I still reach to you
My hands, and through you
Gain things which are, by the things which seem.

TERRA INÇOGNITA.

A LITTLE song has come to me,
A strain of sadness from over sea;
And I hear its music, and love it well,
Though the heart which framed it I cannot tell.

A little picture comes to me,
A dash of brightness from over sea;
There are clasping hands and a holy face –
But the name of the artist who can trace?

So I, in faith which comes to me,
Believe in a land across the sea,
Where my vaguest fancies may stand supreme
In a grand perfection beyond my dream.

O land unknown! in thee alone
Shall formless lyrics to shape be grown;
In thee all rhapsody riseth true,
And the thoughts of beauty are ever new.

O land unknown! where all is best,
In thee is my aspiration blest;
For I toil and tarry until I may
With my broken sentences pass away.

FROM UHLAND.

"Ich hör' meinen Schatz."

My true-love I hear!
  He's swinging his hammer,
  Whose clinking and clamor
  Far outward are rolling
  Like chapel-bells tolling
Where walls interfere.

Though black is the place
  Where labors my lover,
  Yet, as I pass over,
  The bellows are blowing,
  The flames are all glowing
To show me his face.

TWO OF A TRADE.

THE dragon-fly and I together
Sail up the stream in the summer weather;
  He at the stern all green and gold,
  And I at the oars, our course to hold.

Above the floor of the level river
The bent blades dip and spring and quiver;
  And the dragon-fly is here and there,
  Along the water and in the air.

And thus we go as the sunshine mellows,
A pair of nature's merriest fellows;
  For the Spanish cedar is light and true,
  And instead of one, it has carried two.

And thus we sail without care or sorrow,
With trust for to-day and hope for to-morrow;
  He at the stern, all green and gold,
  And I at the oars, our course to hold.

THE LOST SONG.

THERE went a bird away from me,
In the stormy winter, across the sea;
One sudden day,
All chill and gray,
Unto new lands it flew away.

It took from hence, beneath its wing,
One of the songs I used to sing —
A song more sweet
Than I can meet,
Wandering on with weary feet.

But spring has come, and now once more
Hither it flutters as before —
More dear to me
Than these can be,
Because it has flown across the sea.

PAGE AND PAGEANT.

My lord has revels to-night,
  High revel in hall and at board;
His castle flames up with light,
  Which into the night is poured.
And the cressets flare on the tower,
  And the music plays within;
For a chevalier rules the hour,
  Who comes a lady to win.

And I am a page — no more
  Than this — with a plume in my cap,
A lute on my arm, and a store
  Of ballads; and by good hap
Was chosen long since to be
  The minstrel to stay beside
My lady, and bend the knee
  Before this expectant bride.

What business was it of theirs
  How swiftly her glances flew;
Who studies my heart or cares
  When the song and the dance are through?
Who dreams that a page can soar
  In thought as high as a lord,
Or counts me possessed of lore
  Surpassing my lute and sword?

And here am I in the dark,
  While they in the fullest blaze
Are strolling, and I can mark
  Each diamond's lance-like rays;
And she is there with the rest,
  And her knight all silk and plume —
But she is the fairest and best
  Of any who pace the room.

Ah! yes, it is over now:
  There were times when I thought of her
That she bent her beautiful brow
  With love on her worshipper.
But this is a lord of France,
  Some noble of high degree,
Far better fitted to dance
  Attendance than I can be.

Yes, yes, they are calling! Hark!
  There 's my lord with his bulldog bass,
Bellowing through the park,
  And the servants are all in chase
Of me! They would like to hear
  Some Troubadour song, no doubt —
Well, I 'm under the fern; I fear
  They will never find me out.

They have given me up. I thought
  They would come to that very soon,
Though my lord has shouted and sought
  By the light of the harvest moon.

Good-by, old palace of mine,
  Where I sang so many a strain;
The days of the past were fine,
  But I'm off to the world again.

WOVEN ON QUIET DAYS.

THE PALMER'S PREACHING.

I STOOD in a dim old city—
  A city of other days,
With many a stately minster
  Amid its quaint by-ways.

And there, as I gazed and lingered,
  A motley throng passed by—
The knight in his scarlet mantle
  The queen with her pageantry.

The 'prentice went merrily onward,
  And jostled among the best,
With the burgher, secure in his riches,
  And the judge, in his ermine dressed.

The beauty and fame of the city
  Came ever before my eyes;
And I read, in their passing faces,
  Of the wealthy, the proud, the wise.

And it seemed, as they still moved onward,
  Honored or rich or gay,
That a voice bade me give attention
  To a palmer beside the way.

He was sad, and bowed with his travel,
  And his face had a weary look;
While beneath his arm he carried
  An old and sacred book.

He paused by the wayside, gazing
  At the crowd as it swept along,
And he leant on his staff and pondered,
  (It was just at the even-song.)

A look as of holy pity
  Came slowly across his face,
And the rays of the sun enrobed him
  With a halo of saintly grace.

And he stepped him before the passers,
  And, raising his wasted hand,
Stayed all who had sought to hasten,
  With a motion of calm command.

And then from his book he read them
  Of One who came down to earth,
And how He had bled and suffered,
  And how they despised His worth.

And the knight grew pale as he listened;
I could hear the lady sigh;
And the burgher at last bethought him
Of riches laid up on high.

Then the palmer's face grew grander
With the gleam of a saintly love,
As he spoke of a Holy City,
Of a crown that was kept above.

And the multitude stood in silence,
And hearkened, as if for life:
The lady forgot her lover,
The soldier forgot his strife.

And when the palmer ended,
And lifted his hands in prayer,
Stood tears upon many faces,
Which seldom had gathered there.

And while the red of the evening
Closed over the fading day,
With better thoughts and intentions
The multitude went its way.

. . . . . .

It seemed as if night and morning
Came up and across the land,
As again by the crowded pathway
I thought that I took my stand.

And the burgher and judge passed by me,
  And joked as they walked along;
And the song of the merry 'prentice
  Outsounded the even-song.

The lady in silk and jewels,
  The knight in his trappings gay,
The throng of the other evening
  Again came along the way.

And the palmer stood there in silence
  With his book and his carven shell;
For of all who had left him weeping,
  None heeded the lesson well.

THE SPHYNX.

In the midst of the desert sands,
Despising the wasted lands
Which stretch from between her hands,
  She raises her silent form —
Smitten with scath and scar,
By winds which come from afar,
Laden, as tempests are,
  With horrors of howling storm.

What have I to do with thee,
Thou phantom of mystery?
For shapes of the years to be
  Are better than ages past.
How gladly I then would turn
From questions which blanch and burn,
As matters of no concern,
  As things which are not to last!

They may not, they cannot cease
So soon, though all else be peace,
And the concords of time increase
  With the ends of the world on men;
For the problem of fate and chance —
Of life, in the years' advance,
Made captive by circumstance —
  Is bitterer now than then.

12

And the face of that awful one
Whose work has not yet been done,
Outwatching both storm and sun,
  Is full of the question still.
For what is our life at best?—
Is it a way unto rest,
Is it a sneer or a jest,
  Or is it a grasp of the will?

Not thus was the answer told
To deserts of heat or cold,
Nor written in books of gold
  For centuries yet to read;
Since only a chosen few
Have sifted the false and true—
Have seen that the old was new,
  That the riddle was solved indeed.

But the strength of their arms is naught
To conquer the blindness, wrought
Into this stony thought
  By many a mallet-blow;
Until, at the last, a day
Shall burst on the lands with sway,
Sweeping all doubts away
  As gloom at the morning glow.

And the word is a word of pain—
A promise of loss, for gain;
A promise of seed, for grain,

To all who will truth receive.
But, after, comes gain for loss,
When harvests merrily toss,
When Crown shall succeed to Cross;
And the word is the word "Believe!"

CIVITAS DEI.

"For my brethren and companions' sakes I will now say, Peace be within thee!"

City of God, grown old with silent faces
Lying beneath the shadow of the clay,
Thine are the towers built up in barren places,
Thine the great bastions waiting for the day.

Dim through the night stone after stone arises,
Bold through the dawn step forth the peaks of flame,
Touched with the splendor of those glad surprises
By which the blessing of the Spirit came.

Toilers of truth are we, who at our labor
Keep the sharp sword still girded at the thigh,
Heeding no summons of the pipe and tabor,
Fighting and building till the end be nigh.

Much do these walls have need of earnest valor,
Much have they need of plummet and of line,
From early morning clad in whitest pallor,
Until the redness of the day's decline.

Help us, our God! while men with keen derision
Mock our slight structure as it riseth up;
Give them reward of wrath, a fearful vision,
A bitter drinking of an evil cup.

Help us, our God! Despised are we, and broken
  By many sorrows which the wicked cause:
Turn Thou on them their malice, as the token
  Of Thine unerring, unevaded laws.

Thus, then, we build through storm and pleasant weather;
  Thus, then, we pray by morning and by night;
Heart knit with heart, and hands at work together —
  Beset by foes until Thou givest light.

City of God! thy peace is our petition;
  City of God! our brethren dwell in thee;
And for their sakes, in true and deep contrition,
  We seek thy good, O dwelling of the free!

THREE IN ONE.

GREAT was the mystery to me
How Three were One and One was Three—
How God alone was Trinity!

I read it, but it seemed no more
Than breakers sounding on the shore,
From deeps I dreaded to explore:

Until the certainty grew mine
That, somewhere, God had left a sign—
Some symbol perfect and divine.

And, seeking after this, one day
The summer storm-clouds cleared away
In sudden glory, ray on ray:

While there, serene across the sky,
The bow of promise shone on high,
God's token that He cannot lie.

Enlightened by a truth sublime,
I saw this miracle of time,
This wonder known in every clime.

And, fading each to each, I caught
The perfect symbol of my thought—
Three chiefest colors, interwrought.

Three colors in gradations fair,
Which, mingled ever in the air,
Bestow what light we daily share.

For thus I saw the mystery,
And God had left a sign to me
How Three were One and One was Three.

WHENCE AND WHITHER.

I KNOW not whence it comes to me,
  This longing, vague and strange,
For lands across the summer sea,
  Beyond the thought of change —
I know it not, I know it not,
But still it comes to me.

I know not whence the visions drift,
  On sunny days or dark;
Through what white cloud, what fleecy rift
  They fell, I cannot mark —
I know it not, I know it not,
But still they come to me.

I know not where the words are found
  I fashion in my song;
What mansion in the blue profound
  Has held or holds them long —
I know it not, I know it not,
But still they come to me.

I know not where the end shall be
  To these, my hopes and dreams,
Until the happy land I see,
  Where all is as it seems —
I know it not, I know it not,
Until it comes to me.

THE DISTANT KING.

My lord, whom I would fain obey,
Has left his realm and gone away;

But he committed to my hand
More things than I could understand.

He gave to me the golden keys
Of honors, ranks, and dignities;

He placed a book before my sight
Wherein my heart itself may write;

He opened wide a secret door
Where wealth and wisdom are in store;

He clad me with a robe of grace,
And set me in his vacant place;

To me he left his seal of state,
With counsels of exceeding weight.

"All things are yours," my master saith,
"Save the control of life and death."

And therefore I, reflecting still
Upon my absent master's will,

Am watchful, both with hand and brain,
Until his feet return again.

And still there rests upon my mind
A thought of what is unresigned;

For powers of life and death must be
His mighty master-works with me.

He holds them balanced for my sight,
Sorrow and comfort, dark and bright.

And so I wait and work and pray
While my dear lord remains away,

That at his coming he may give
His last best gift — the right to live!

"PULVIS ET UMBRA SUMUS."

"Two handfuls of white dust shut in an urn of brass."
TENNYSON.

No more than this? To die and fade
Into a shade?
To be at last, whate'er our worth,
But dust of earth?

No more than this? To pass away
From light and day?
To be but ashes at the best,
An urn our rest?

No more than this? No hope to cheer
The lonely bier?
No trust when this our life is o'er,
To meet once more?

Yes, more than this! — a future rest
Among the blest;
Where, garlanded with asphodel,
We still may dwell.

Yes, more than this! To him who stands
On higher lands,
These dim forebodings cease to be
Eternity!

Yes, more than this! No heathen sage
Of any age
May dull the ears which once have heard
The Better Word.

PAULLUS OR PAUL?

"Animæ magnæ prodigum Paullum." — HORACE.

"I count not my life dear unto myself." — ST. PAUL.

HEATHEN and Christian together!
  Lo! how their courages meet;
Bravely determining whether
  One can the other defeat.

Paullus — or Paul the Apostle?
  Jove the Supreme — or the One
Born near the crowd of an hostel,
  Claimed for the Deity's Son?

Which is most truly heroic:
  Bravery purchasing fame?
Or, with the grace of a Stoic,
  Parting with honor and name?

Striving for chaplets of laurel,
  Won by the sheerest of force?
Or, far aloof from the quarrel,
  Tracing life up to its source?

Unto the one shall be given
  Guerdon of earthly renown,
While for the other, in heaven,
  Waits an unchangeable crown.

Which shall we honor as hero:
  Him whom the Latins adored?
Or the one martyred by Nero,
  Dying for love of his Lord?

Heathen and Christian together!
  Let it be rightly confessed
Glory is fleeting, and whether
  Earth can afford us the best.

EVANUIT.

I TREAD the withered leaves beneath my feet,
  Above my head they crown the wood with gold;
For here the summer and the autumn meet,
  And the old story of the year is told
    To wood and wold.

The blossoms pass through beauty to decay;
  The rich, full green grows gilded in the sun;
Their strength and favor gently fade away
  Before the warm, bright days are fairly done
    Or snows begun.

The haze of Indian summer on the hills
  Hangs tenderly and like a vail of gauze,
Through which all beauty even more fulfils
  The grand yet viewless motion of the laws
    Of its First Cause.

And all things pass to death. Ah, is it so,
  That Time must tread them underneath his feet?
Must blast them with his cruel breath, although
  They come not to perfection, as is meet
    In things so sweet?

And must these leaves fly off before the storm?
  These leaves, so like unto our withered days,
Dying in sunlight beautiful and warm,
  Decaying in these cheerful autumn rays
    Like transient praise.

Yet be it glory even unto these,
  That the great mother Earth receives them all —
Aye, even as our bodies when it please
  Our Father God that we, as leaves, should fall
      When He doth call.

And be it glory to their lesser lot
  That they shall not be lost so utterly —
Aye, even as ourselves, for may we not,
  O Lord of Hosts, be useful unto Thee
      Eternally?

Farewell, O withered leaves! the tale is told,
  The old, sad tale of winter and of frost;
The story which our eyes so much behold,
  Of beauty lavished, and the final cost
      Of glory, lost.

AT THE SABBATH'S CLOSE.

INTO the garner of the past
  My day has gone;
  Its work has all been done,
Its seed been cast.

Whether to good or yet to ill
  Its toil shall tend,
  Thou knowest, Heavenly Friend:
My trust fulfil.

Out of such empty air create
  Some thoughts divine,
  Kindled by word of mine —
These consecrate.

Saviour, supremest, best,
  Receive my day,
  And hear me when I pray
In Thee to rest.

So, in the quiet of the night
  I lay me down,
  Thy work my noblest crown,
My chief delight.

THALATTA! THALATTA!

THE days which went so long ago,
  Have come again to me,
As now I tread, with footstep slow,
  The margin of the sea.

The little ripples breaking in
  Crawl gently up the sand,
Whose shifting masses seek to win
  Their kingdom from the land.

A stranded shell, a bit of weed,
  A slope of carven beach—
In such old characters I read
  Of what the Past can teach.

For change has been and change is not
  (Since all is still the same)—
Nor do I reach the pleasant spot
  To which my boyhood came.

Farewell, O Past!—the ocean surge
  Has torn and swept away
The ragged bluffs, the grassy verge
  On which I used to play.

And here I stand, a man indeed,
  Upon another shore,
With other shells and other weed
  Than I have seen before.

Far out, the waters inward. bound
  Lift lines and crests of foam;
Beyond them all I have not found
  The rest and peace of home.

Send unto me, O changeless Past,
  Some word of hope and strength,
Which, through these changes new and vast,
  Shall bear my soul at length.

For so the waters plunge and sway
  While storm and tide shall be,
Until we pass, some happy day,
  Across the Tideless Sea.

DREAMING.

In the quiet afternoon,
  As the rain drops softly down,
  And the tree-trunks, wet and brown,
  Stand like sentries of the town —
Then the light fades off too soon,
For my heart is all in tune.

Then I hear each gentle sound
  From the leaves which stir again
  At the touches of the rain;
  And the moisture on the pane,
Slowly rolling to the ground,
Has some sweet expression found.

On the unjust and the just
  Falls this benison the same,
  Blessing, in the Father's name,
  Home of love and haunt of shame,
Cleansing off the gathered dust
From a long-neglected trust.

And I dream, I know not why,
  Of all peaceful things and sad —
  All the hopes my life has had
  Since they dwelt with me, a lad
From whose sight this darker sky
Hid the perfect realms on high.

Now I wait in all content,
  Whether skies be dark or bright;
  Morning follows after night,
  Darkness will be changed to light;
And when days of storm are spent,
There shall be a rainbow sent.

So the leaves may quiver still
  At the touches of the rain;
  So the moisture on the pane
  May be scattered or remain:
These shall yet in peace fulfil
Unto me that Better Will.

THE PAIR-OAR.

Comrade mine, as we row along
  By the fresh, green banks where the willows grow,
Let the pulse of our stroke be true and strong
  From the bent blades flickering to and fro.

Sharp the prow as it cuts away,
  In a wedge-like furrow, the level stream;
And the wrinkles run from the dropping spray
  As our bright spruce pinions dart and gleam.

Bubbles swell from the shining track
  Of our keel and the oar-strokes flaring wide,
And the wake of foam runs merrily back,
  With its tiny eddies on either side.

"Now avast!" and we lightly float
  Into shadow and coolness, where the trees
Are a mighty arbor above our boat,
  And the oars hang gently and drift at ease.

Then once more through the open strait
  Of the fresh, green banks where the willows grow,
On the homeward stretch — with a glance elate
  At the bent blades flickering to and fro.

Comrade mine of the old pair-oar,
  Are there days of a better joy than this,
When we slip so swiftly beside the shore
  With our strokes as true as our friendship is?

Never long will the daylight last,
  Or the Spring of the happy year endure —
Let us catch the pleasures which hurry past,
  While our arms are strong and our stroke is sure.

"IVSTITIA."

A POOR, bruised statue, on a Venice column,
Which has no grace except the grace of name,
And yet whose features, worn and sad and solemn,
Put the long record of the Past to shame.

A battered face, whose beauty has departed;
An artist's dream, which had its ending here;
A hope, which faded even as it started,
A joy, which found fulfilment in a fear.

But still no time destroys what once was spoken,
No years can alter the Divine decree;
Though Justice suffer, and her rule be broken,
The day has come when Venice shall be free.

Not now a statue beaten by the ages;
Not now a record of an evil Past;
Her glory shall illumine all the pages
Where the dark shade of tyranny was cast.

1867.

FAIRY-TALES.

To E. P., Jr., 1867.

My little friend with the golden hair
  Rests his head on my arm to-night,
As we sit at ease in the great arm-chair
  Under the softly-shaded light.

And wonderful fancies come and go
  Over the depths of his dreamy eyes:
They are tokens of thoughts which spread and grow
  Into a manhood strong and wise.

He knows not yet, this beautiful child,
  The things which trouble an older brain;
How the heart of his youth may be defiled
  Searching for praise or planning gain.

But now he rests, with his golden hair,
  Safe on my arm whom doubts assail:
He has yet his battle to fight with care:
  All to him is a fairy-tale.

And what to him are the waiting days
  In which these pitiful lives go on?
What does he know of a thousand ways,
  Evil and worse, beneath the sun?

Ah! long may it be until he learns
  That fairy visions are ended quite,
That the wonders which now his heart discerns
  Never are seen by clearer light.

And long may it be ere time erase
  The traces of that which fades too soon,
When the golden moments shall lose their grace
  Under the glare of a sultry noon.

THE TWO HEAVENS.

הַשָּׁמַיִם

—*Biblia Hebraica.*

We make to ourselves a gladness,
  A joy like the one above,
When the toil of each daily duty
  Shall be wholly done from love.

Around us shall spread a heaven,
  Be we never so weak and faint,
As the hallowing rays encircle
  The brows of some pictured saint.

And yet, how we fail in trial!
  How sternly the duties rise!
Till it seems that their hated presence
  Would darken the very skies.

Ah! were there no other heaven
  Save this which has changed so soon,
The sky were indeed but darkness,
  The sun had gone down at noon.

Yet hearken, O sick with labor,
  O furrowed and bent with care,
Not here is the better heaven,
  But far in another air.

The rays of a higher glory
  Shall render this toil sublime,
And lift into endless ages
  The work we have wrought for time.

And so may the days be precious,
  Though we wait to enter there,
And the very heaven of heavens
  May be over us everywhere.

Through the clouds that are round about us
  We look to the upper day,
And the golden sun, at his coming,
  Shall gather them all away.

THE NAME IN THE BARK.

IN the bark of a silver-poplar tree,
  With the first good knife that I ever had,
(Thinking, perhaps, of destiny,
  And the days of the future, bright or sad,)
I carved initials which mark my name,
And left what answered as well as fame.

I was a boy, and the bark was hard;
  The forms of the letters had not grown
Into a symmetry fit to guard
  What I committed to them alone;
And so the hopes of my youth were there,
Clumsy and straggling and rude and bare.

Many a day had I left the spot,
  To seek for a knowledge of higher things;
With the broken knife-blades I forgot
  The fame which lifted me on its wings;
But the tree stood up in the mellow light,
And grew with my growth by morn and night.

After awhile I came again
  To see the faces I used to see —
To hear old voices — and I was fain
  To visit also the poplar-tree;
For I viewed it across the village street,
Where parsonage-garden and pasture meet.

Ah, me! the letters were there indeed —
  Those rough boy-carvings of other days;
Widened as much as had been my creed,
  But failing to merit a word of praise;
Burst by the force of the swelling trunk,
Yet all of their beauty sadly shrunk.

I looked long moments upon them there,
  And my heart was full of a heavy pain;
For I thought of the labor and the care
  Which cut them out on the silver grain;
And I said, "How little we really know
Into what shapes our lives may grow!

"These fair devices which suit us well,
  Which seem to the boy such a perfect thought,
May change and sever, and none can tell
  Into what fashion they are wrought:
And the man comes by, and says, 'Can this be
The figure of that which was dear to me?'"

O boy and man! on the smooth, white bark
  Of the days of our years there are many words,
Which shine phosphoric within the dark,
  Or even have music like the birds';
But happy is he who, with steady art,
Cuts the great word GOD on his growing heart.

GROPINGS.

"What shall we say but that the vestiges of immortality impressed upon man are absolutely indelible?" —CALVIN, *Inst.* I., *cap.* v.

WHAT shall we say, if through our lives
  A golden bond divine may run
  Which links our diverse minds to One,
Howe'er this baser heart contrives?

The mysteries we know not here,
  The phantoms which escape our hand,
  The hope of some long-promised land—
Shall all through this be rendered clear?

Shall this return us back to God
  Diviner than we dreamed to be—
  This fadeless immortality
Which bears with us each earthly load?

Are we but battle-grounds at best,
  Whereon contend two shapes unknown,
  Each striving for the central throne,
In conflict which can give no rest?

Or do we reach to either side
  And make of one our firm ally—
  Although we choose scarce knowing why—
And thus our fears are satisfied?

Are we but driven here and there
  With this bright jewel on our breast,
  Of which we are not dispossessed
By years of sin, or doubt, or care?

Shall we arise at last by this,
  And be in purer realms discerned,
  Like unto those who long have learned
The way of Heaven's eternal bliss?

Or shall we sink it far from sight,
  Forget, and crush it out of mind,
  That, as we leave its claims behind,
It shall debar us from the light?

O answer this, proud soul, to me!
  Shalt thou go drifting down the sky,
  Or spread broad wings of faith and fly
Upward to Him who fashioned thee?

A SPRING DAY.

MAY 10TH, 1868.

METHINKS I worshipped God to-day
After my own especial way;
For all the air with the early bloom
Was laden, and Nature's busy loom
Had shifted its pattern into lines
Of long green tendrils and twining vines.
The branches quivered with leaves anew;
The springing blossoms had broken through,
And over the road an apple-bough
Had flaked them off like a storm just now.
The Sabbath stillness crept all across
Under the woods and on the moss;
The quiet light of the sunset came,
Bearing a message still the same;
A bird that twittered above my head
Sang of the Father's daily bread;
I felt cool grasses beneath my feet,
And smelt the violets faint and sweet;
And each replied, as it best could tell
Of the hand which had made and loved it well.
I may have dreamed, but it seemed to me
That I heard the same from a loaded bee,
And even the rustle of the woods
Spoke of those pathless solitudes
Where the same hand, by day and night,
Labors and fashions and plans aright.

And so with the rest I sang my song
Of Him unto whom we all belong,
And my heart, though once it was dark with doubt,
Turned the old shapes of darkness out;
For I felt that the Lord of the world, who kept
Watch of His work while others slept,
Would surely scatter abroad in me
The seeds for His own eternity—
Would gather and garner from all my deeds
Some little wheat out of many weeds.
And whether I praised Him well or no
I cannot tell, but a sudden glow
Struck to my soul, as though One divine
Laid His pierced hand in this hand of mine.

WEEDS.

THOUGH we turn the furrow with care and pain,
Though we break the clods of the yielding soil,
Let but the land unwatched remain,
And weeds are the end of all our toil.

How deep soever we drive the plough,
The evil principles there abide;
We know not why they have come nor how,
Nor why from air and from light they hide.

Feathery seeds of the dandelion,
Thistle-blows thick for a future stock,
Purslain and chickweed and poison-vine,
Unendurable yellow dock;

Rankest weeds of disgrace are they,
Changing to evil our best intent,
Making the choicest of crops decay,
Letting our labor be idly spent.

Ah! if only our lives were free
Of these analogies sad and dark!
Ah, if only our hearts might be
Clean of this curse which we sternly mark!

Could we but furrow the surface clay,
Farming the soil of our souls aright!
Could we but tend it a single day,
And know that it must our toil requite!

Could we do this! And yet not so
  Has our great Husbandman long designed;
His is the order that we must know,
  The inner as well as the outer mind.

And thus from day unto day we strive,
  And thus from day unto day we wait,
Seeking to keep our grain alive
  By weeding early and weeding late.

Faith has promised a happy time
  When toil and sorrow at last are o'er,
When the grain has grown in a favored clime,
  And care is ended for evermore.

Then shall the reaping be broad and grand;
  Then shall our patience be well repaid;
Then from the charge of a cheerful land,
  The long-watched harvest aside be laid.

MY PREACHER.

THE Sabbath work is over and done,
  The cares of the day at length are ended;
The light has faded, and with the sun
  The solemn splendor of God was blended—
But still I wait, for I long to hear
The voice of one speaking full and clear.

I weary at words which seem too poor
  And faint and feeble amid their fashion,
Which never attain a height so sure
  As draws the world from its pride and passion:
Myself—and only myself—I hear;
Not one who is speaking full and clear.

The marvellous truth of Holy Writ,
  Which deepens and widens in its meaning,
Abashes me when I talk of it
  As though no spaces were intervening:
Only a common voice I hear,
Far other than that which is full and clear.

Therefore a man of God shall come
  Out of my shelves, and give me warning;
Give comfort, now that I long for some,
  Or teach me meekness instead of scorning—
A preacher of Christ, who in my ear
Shall tell of a truth both full and clear.

And he and I, as the midnight nears,
  As over the earth a stillness hovers,
Shall find an ending to many fears
  Under the guard of these dusty covers.
This is the man whom I can hear —
His are the messages full and clear.

O Preacher of mine, whom, long ago,
  The Lord of Hosts to Himself hath taken,
I read with reverence, for I know
  Even as I am thou wast shaken.
In highest honor I hold thee dear,
For thou hast been speaking full and clear.

IN DARKNESS.

We spend our years as an idle tale —
  A tale that is told ere the years go by;
We plan and labor and yield and fail,
  And then — pass into the boundless sky.

Whither hence shall we bend our way,
  Or whither hence shall we follow on?
And will there then be another day
  After the night of our life is gone?

Poor, faint heart! — and thou dost not see
  The light which shines on thy darkest time,
Which casts a radiance yet for thee
  From hidden depths of a further clime?

Trust and toil, and the end will come,
  With brightness better for long delay,
With heralding better than trump or drum,
  And glory which never shall fade away.

AD MEIPSUM.

Had I the words which weave and twine
  Around dull things with nature's art —
Or if the gift were only mine
  By some old power to touch the heart —
Then would I sit and catch the notes
Which birds upraise with happy throats,
  And mine should be the happier art.

O master-singer! far away
  Thy strong, free pinions bore thee on;
We only wait, and sadly say,
  "The old heroic times are gone."
We strike the strings with feeble hand,
We wake no long-unheeding land,
  Though we are many, Thou art One.

Music? This measure cannot reach
  Those clear, sweet heights of sound serene;
I fail with all the rest, and teach
  No better souls to stand between
The throng, who look with eager eyes
On unavailing Paradise,
  And them who tread that fadeless green.

But if God grant me now and then
  A verse from some dear angel's book —

If He shall help me upward, when
  It may be given that I look,
For one brief moment, at the plan
Framed with the earth as time began,
  That shall seem better which I took.

And even as a child may tell
  Of hidden and mysterious things,
I, too, may utter passing well
  Our longings, and the inward stings
Which, unto every heart of man
Born with our being, under ban,
  Forever this existence brings.

Then, if the breath of some new thought
  Thrills the slow music of the time —
If hopes of higher help are brought
  Out of another, purer clime —
If men grow better, and their hearts
Lighten, through this, the best of arts,
  I shall have prospered with my rhyme.

SHREDS AND TAGS.

DIES IRÆ.

I.

DAY of wrath, thine awful morning
 Burns to ashes earth's adorning,
As the saint and seer give warning.

II.

Then what terror of each nation
When the Judge shall take His station,
Strictly trying His creation!

III.

When the trumpet-tone of thunder,
Bursting bands of tombs asunder,
Bids men face that throne of wonder.

IV.

Death and Nature He surprises,
Who, a creature, yet arises
Unto those most dread assizes.

V.

There that written book remaineth
Whose sure registry containeth
That which all the world arraigneth.

VI.

Therefore, when He judgeth rightly,
We shall view each act unsightly:
Nothing shall be pardoned lightly.

VII.

With what answer shall I meet Him,
By what advocate entreat him,
When the just may scarcely greet Him?

VIII.

King of mightiest coronation,
Some through grace gain approbation —
Save me, Source of all salvation!

IX.

Hear me, O thou Holy Saviour,
Brought to earth through my behavior —
Take not then away Thy favor.

X.

Seeking me, Thy love outwore Thee,
And the cross, my ransom, bore Thee:
Let not this seem light before Thee.

XI.

Righteous Judge of my condition,
Grant me, for my sins, remission,
Ere the day which ends contrition.

XII.

In my guilt, for pity yearning,
With my shame my face is burning;
Spare me, Lord, to Thee returning!

XIII.

Thou, once touched by Mary's crying,
Who didst save the thief, though dying,
Gavest hope to me when sighing.

XIV.

Poorly are my prayers ascending,
But do Thou, in mercy bending,
Leave me not to flames unending.

XV.

Give me with Thy sheep a station,
Far from goats in separation —
On Thy right my habitation.

XVI.

When the wicked meet conviction,
Doomed to fires of sharp affliction,
Call me forth with benediction.

XVII.

Now I pray Thee, naught commending,
Flames of pride to ashes tending:
Guard me then when earth is ending.

XVIII.

O that day so full of weeping,
When, in dust no longer sleeping,
Man must face his worst behavior;
Therefore, spare me, God and Saviour!

THE IDEALS.

"Und wilt du treulos," etc. — SCHILLER.

AND wilt thou, faithless, from me sever,
  With fancies which were once so sweet,
With all thy griefs and joys, and never
  Relenting, stay thy rapid feet?
Can nothing hold thee as thou fliest,
  O golden time of life, for me?
In vain! thy surge sweeps ever highest,
  Into the vast, eternal sea!

Gone are those suns which shone so brightly,
  Which cheered for me my youthful way;
And those Ideals sink as lightly,
  Which once my heart could not allay.
For it is fled, that sweet confiding
  In nature which produced my dream,
And now, before the world's harsh chiding,
  Godlike and fair no more shall seem.

As once, with deep and strong devotion,
  Pygmalion embraced the stone,
Till in its marble cheek the motion
  Of life in glowing rapture shone —
So did I throw, with youthful yearning,
  About the earth a lover's arm,
Till, on my poet-bosom burning,
  She breathed and moved, becoming warm;

And sharing these my fond caresses,
  She who was dumb found speech at last,
Repaid again my loving kisses,
  And read my fancies as they passed.
Then did the trees and flowers adore me,
  Then sang to me the waterfall
In silver notes, while round and o'er me
  I found my echoed life in all.

How strives the weak and struggling spirit
  To grasp the world which rims it round,
To try this life upon its merit
  In thought and word, in shape and sound!
How rare appeared this earthly fashion
  So long as in the bud it grew!
How poor and worthy of compassion
  The feeble bloom it tended to!

How springs, by lofty courage hastened,
  The youth upon the path of life,
Whose dreams no sorrow yet has chastened,
  Or proved them with delusion rife!
Up in the limits of the ether
  His eye discerns the palest star;
His soaring fancy bears him thither
  On wings which seek the high and far.

How lightly is he onward speeding!
  What can be hard to one so free?
While still before Life's steeds unheeding
  Dance on a merry company.

Here's Love which knows no vexing quarrel,
  Here's Fortune with her golden crown,
Here's Glory with his wreath of laurel,
  And Truth on whom the sun shines down.

Yet, ah! midway upon the journey
  The comrades turn their steps aside;
They are but faithless in the tourney,
  They fail so soon as each is tried.
Swift-footed Happiness is vanished,
  The soul thirsts on unsatisfied;
By doubt's dark cloud the light is banished,
  And Truth's bright form is undescried.

I saw the holy crown of Glory
  Debased upon a worthless brow;
Alas! how short proved Love's glad story;
  Its brief, rich spring is perished now.
And thus it stiller grew, and ever
  Deserted stretched the rugged way;
Hope trembled at my side, and never
  Shed in advance a cheering ray.

Of all the joyous comrades by me,
  Who stays with loving glances yet?
Who stands yet true and trusting nigh me,
  And follows till my sun be set?
Dear Friendship, thou alone, who healest
  My wounds with soft and tender hand,
Who all my cares and burdens feelest,
  Whom early I could understand.

And thou, brave Labor, who so gladly
  Canst aid to calm the heaving breast,
Who buildest joyfully or sadly,
  Destroying naught, nor needing rest—
Thou who to those eternal ages
  Givest but these poor grains we seem,
And yet, through whom, Time's guilty pages
  These moments, days, and years redeem.

THE BREAKING OF THE THREAD.

THESE have I woven.— Thou dost know,
Dear Only One, how often here
The patterns on the fabric grow
In the old shapes of day and year;
How often, watching friend and foe,
I made their faces reappear.

To thee each story of the past,
Dug from a dusty book or brain,
Has memories upon it cast
To make the dim illusion plain:
The sun is as we saw it last;
The fresh Spring-days return again.

O wondrous web of human life!
Thy Warp and Woof of circumstance,
Now bright with calm or dark with strife,
Has felt the rapid shuttle glance,
And known the days with fancies rife,
And watched design contend with chance.

The thoughts which crowded took the pen—
That wondrous shuttle—flying in

And out among the ways of men;
Which caught such patterns as begin
Where hearts are best, and wove them when
The other looms had ceased their din.

Thou Only One, to thee alone
Such things are opened, sure and true—
As well these fancies of my own
As those which former workmen drew:
Take then the things which thou hast known,
Take the whole fabric, old and new!

www.ingramcontent.com/pod-product-compliance
Lightning Source LLC
LaVergne TN
LVHW011236110826
845150LV00006B/1654